THE WOMAN WHO DISCOVERED PRINTING

T. H. BARRETT

THE WOMAN WHO DISCOVERED PRINTING

Yale University Press
NEW HAVEN AND LONDON

For information about this and other Yale University Press publications, please contact:

U.S. Office: sales.press@yale.edu   www.yalebooks.com
Europe Office: sales@yaleup.co.uk   www.yaleup.co.uk

Set in Minion by J&L Composition, Filey, North Yorkshire
Printed in Great Britain by Cambridge University Press

Library of Congress Cataloguing-in-Publication Data

Barrett, Timothy Hugh.
  The woman who discovered printing/T.H. Barrett.
    p. cm.
  Includes bibliographical references and index.
  ISBN 978–0–300–12728–7 (alk. paper)
    1. Printing—China—History—Origin and antecedents. 2. Printing—History—Origin and antecedents. 3. Wu hou, Empress of China, 624-705.
  I. Title.
  Z186.C5B37 2007
  686.209—dc22
                                                        2007027346

A catalogue record for this book is available from the British Library

10 9 8 7 6 5 4 3 2 1

CONTENTS

ILLUSTRATIONS

A NOTE ON TRANSCRIPTION AND SOURCES

For Chinese this book uses the pinyin transcription, even though this results in some unfamiliar forms, such as 'Tang' for 'T'ang' as the name of the dynasty ruled over by the Li family, and 'Yangzi' for 'Yangtze' as the name of the river. The ancient sage Laozi, reputed author of the *Daode jing*, is none other than the sage formerly known as Lao-tze, author of the *Tao Te Ching*. I have, however, baulked at calling the religious tradition he is supposed to have founded 'Daoism', as many North American colleagues do, in favour of the better-established 'Taoism', since the former term is still new enough to cause confusion amongst the unwary, while the latter is still deliberately espoused by some of my own colleagues and is in any case still better known outside the academic community.

Though the footnotes occasionally name what I take to be well-known editions of standard Chinese texts, I have tried to avoid too many references to sources in Chinese, preferring wherever possible to cite the more technical articles in which I have published my research during the past decade, where fuller references to the sources may be found. But putting together these research findings with those of other scholars has involved some fresh discoveries in Chinese Buddhist materials. These may all be located in the major series known as the 'Taisho Canon', which represents the best-known attempt at a critical edition of the vast collection of texts in the Chinese Buddhist canon. Its full title and publication details are as follows: Takakasu Junjirō and Watanabe Kaigyoku, eds, *Taishōshinshūdaizōkyō*. Tokyo: Taishōissaikyōkankōkai, 1924–1932. 100 volumes. Citations are to the pages of the volumes in this series, though I also indicate the fascicle numbers if it seems possible that other editions might be worth consulting, and give the identifying number assigned to each text in the series.

INTRODUCTION AND ACKNOWLEDGEMENTS

This book argues that more than thirteen hundred years ago – over twice as long ago as the time of Johannes Gutenberg in Europe – China had already developed an ability to print on a massive scale. But because the most prominent supporter of this development was a woman, after her death those in authority ignored the technology for a full two centuries. Sheer misogyny was undoubtedly a factor in this, but dynastic politics, religious rivalries, vested scribal interests, elite snobbery and even a whiff of xenophobia also all played a part to a greater or lesser degree. Above all, because Chinese scribal culture, based on paper and the ink brush, was immensely superior to the scribal culture of medieval Europe, printing simply did not have the immediate appeal that it did in the West. Far from answering a crying educational need for more books, printing in China answered a political need for more holy objects. This is such an unfamiliar idea that much of my book is taken up with explaining its background. It is not, however, my argument that the religious concepts associated with this alien (though not entirely alien) notion of holy objects made the development of printing take place more smoothly in China, even though as a way of exploring past modes of thinking I devote some space to religious metaphors concerning the transfer of patterns from one surface to another. Rather, I propose that the historically conditioned desire for more holy objects under a particular set of circumstances made printing an attractive option compared with other technologies for one particular woman, and so brought the practice to more widespread attention for the first time.

In Chapter One I first outline a case for taking Chinese printing seriously, since in much of the English-speaking world our education systems are still Eurocentric enough for many people to have grown up to assume that only Gutenberg's form of printing is of any importance. In Chapter Two I look at some of the background features in China that helped from early times to develop an understanding of printing, though it is not until Chapter Three, when I take up the importation to China of Buddhist ideas, that the reader will encounter the religious beliefs that first inspired printing. In Chapter Four I then look at the religious environment of China in the sixth century. My argument is that it was unusually unstable as the result of a sudden climate change. But even if I am wrong, it is important to see China's rulers not as absolute despots convinced of their own unlimited power, but as all too frail human beings who constantly needed to bolster their authority.

In Chapter Five I then turn to the ruling house of the seventh century, and to the rise to power of one of the imperial consorts who married into the family. It is this woman who is the heroine of our story. But although she is well known to historians of China, I have decided not to use the two names – Empress Wu or Wu Zetian – by which she is generally known. I have referred to her instead by using English versions of the various titles she bore at different times. I will offer some brief explanation of these as they come up in the text, but when in doubt, any capitalised title from the middle chapters onwards will probably be hers. By this means I hope to show something of the variety of public roles she played, before turning in Chapter Six to extraordinary new evidence that both shows something of her own private beliefs, and also strengthens the probability that she would have had a personal interest in mass printing.

In Chapter Seven the focus then shifts, away from a broad description of the intellectual and political environment that produced printing towards something much narrower. For having made a general case, I need to look closely for any evidence that she did what she was apparently minded to do. A detailed examination of the historical record here does not clinch the matter, and neither does a detailed examination in Chapter Eight of the later scraps of evidence that survive for printing in the following century or so: these chapters will certainly be hard going for any reader of history who expects a stream of effortless revelations. Unfortunately, sometimes, when there is nothing much on the record, even a quite meticulous scrutiny cannot establish firm conclusions. But these chapters do have a point in that they allow me in Chapter Nine to step back from the details and look at some broader patterns, and so at least to come up with reasonable hypotheses to explain the apparently erratic development of printing in East Asia.

I hope that these suggestions will prove of some interest, and especially that they will serve as a stimulus to further research. For I feel sure that the findings presented here cannot be taken as definitive, not simply (as I explain further on) because of the constant additions to our knowledge being made by archaeology, but also because I suspect that an even closer analysis of certain key periods may yet add significantly to our knowledge. The emergence to respectability of printing during the late ninth and early tenth centuries still deserves more detailed study, and I intend to devote further work to this phase myself. But a yet more thoroughly comprehensive and detailed examination of the late seventh and early eighth centuries, encompassing all the political and religious developments in China and within the larger Asian context, might in future clarify many of the points that have puzzled me when putting together my remarks.

Any yet more detailed investigation would, however, be unlikely to attract the substantial research funding required to support it without a clearly reasoned statement as to what evidence we have already, and how it may be construed. The purpose of the following pages is therefore to supply for the benefit of future researchers, as much as current readers, a provisional account of how the known facts may be seen in relation to each other, though of course a number of new facts have come to light in the process of writing this account. In particular my aim has been to provide a possible explanation of why the rise of printing in East Asia seems to have followed a course very different from the one it took in Europe; I intend to do this without resorting to *a priori* assumptions about the supposed difficulties of printing the Chinese script, since these assumptions have for far too long discouraged research into Chinese printing by unduly minimising its significance. The outcome of my own work is therefore perhaps a book very different from that which my colleagues may have expected to see, addressed as it is not solely to the select circle of specialists in the early Tang dynasty but to all who may be interested in what is, after all, an important problem in world history. For this I take full responsibility.

I absolve from any blame for the mistakes and inadequacies in my work all those who have been kind enough to offer me their financial or academic support. I'd like to thank my wife, Helen Spillett, ahead even of those who have supported me financially, for without her support and encouragement their money would have been wasted. She has read everything I have written, warning me as a result against any number of confusions and infelicities, and has also travelled with me to both the very centre and the very edge of China in search of present traces of the events and processes I describe. This book is as much hers as mine. I am most grateful, too, to the Arts and Humanities Research Council (as it then was) for supporting an extra term of sabbatical leave that allowed me to complete the longest research article underlying this study, and to the Chiang Ching-kuo Foundation for their generous support of further extended study leave in order to turn several years of sporadic research into the manuscript of the book that you now see before you. This arrangement would have been impossible without the co-operation of the School of Oriental and African Studies, London, and most especially of the then Dean of Humanities, Tom Tomlinson, and without the support of my referees, Glen Dudbridge and Chris Cullen. Constant encouragement from Robert Baldock and Malcolm Gerratt at Yale University Press has also been indispensable.

During the final stages of my research I was particularly grateful for the opportunity to discuss some of my work at the University of Tennessee at Knoxville with Miriam Levering, Hilde de Weerdt and Suzanne Wright and their students, and also at Stanford, thanks to Carl Bielefeldt, Fabrizio Pregadio and Michael Zimmerman. But the erratic progress of my studies has meant that I have accumulated debts to a number of audiences and individuals over a much longer period of time, ever since Florian Reiter first showed me the reference to printed images in his own draft translation of the *Fengdao ke*. A provisional stage was reached with the presentation of some findings at Wolfson College, Oxford, in February 2001, and I am grateful not simply to Glen Dudbridge for his invitation to talk on that occasion but also to Peter Kornicki and Joe McDermott for their subsequent comments on my text. So many other presentations on other occasions crowd together in my memory that it is hard to recall their exact sequence, but conferences of the United Kingdom Association for Buddhist Studies and at St John's College, and visits to the Needham Research Institute, to the Universities of Bristol and British Columbia and the Historical Association as well as to my own department's research seminar were all useful. Although I have tried to acknowledge specific assistance in my notes, the number of friends whose unacknowledged but still helpful remarks remain in my conscious memory – to say nothing of those whose advice I have unconsciously assimilated – now forms quite a long list, which certainly includes James Benn, Chen Jinhua, Chen Jo-shui, Chris Cullen, Ho Peng Yoke, Buzzy Teiser, Richard Salomon, Greg Schopen and Mark Strange. Charles Aylmer, Liu Yi, John Moffett and Zhou Xun were invaluable in securing useful materials for me, while in the final stages of revising my work Antonello Palumbo and Valentina Boretti both gave indispensable advice on the basis of their own unpublished researches. Their exceptional readiness to help reminds me of the great generosity of friends and teachers of earlier times – the late Antonino Forte, Piet van der Loon and Denis Twitchett, and also David McMullen, Tonami Mamoru and Stanley Weinstein, without the example of whose inspiring scholarship even this slight recompense for past kindness would have been impossible. Ultimately, of course, my debts extend to all the friends and family who have encouraged and taught me since infancy, and I am mindful that for their support and love over an even longer period I have correspondingly even less to show than to my friends and teachers in academic life. To those whom I have not seen for a while, this is what I grew up to do. I hope that there will be those who will find what I have to say worth knowing. As for the errors, misconceptions and misstatements, they are nobody's fault but mine.

There are, finally, two ways in which my own institution has given me specific help. I am grateful to my colleagues for awarding me a grant from the funds of the Sino-British Fellowship Trust towards some of my travel in China. I would also like to express my thanks to the Director of SOAS, Professor Paul Webley, in his role as Chairman of the Management Committee of the Percival David Foundation, for agreeing to allow me to use a substantial amount of material from my contribution to the twenty-third of the Foundation's Colloquies on Art and Archaeology in Asia in my opening chapter.

CHAPTER ONE

THE VIEW FROM JARROW

People today are losing touch with the technologies that first made the world they still inhabit. The experience of reading a book, as you are doing right now, is still much the same for you as it was when reading first became an activity in which large numbers of people were able to participate over half a millennium ago. It is the technology that has made the activity possible that has evolved. What most people like to think of as the modern world of print, this world of newspapers and novels, was based originally on no more than the process of pressing ink and paper together so as to create a black and white pattern in the shape of words. Yet that served well enough for hundreds of years, and it is only now that the whole process begins (and, for an increasing number, also ends) on a screen, in an electronic environment far removed from anything that can be touched and felt with our hands.

My cousin, who lived on the other side of the country from us east of London near the sea in Essex, grew up to be a printer, and remembers the days when even the most humble printing task in his locality was carried out by hand – 'winkle bag printing', they called it. But it is years since he used those skills. There are still a few people around who know how to carry out printing the old way, and practise the craft for pleasure as much as profit. For all commercial purposes, though, the long story is at an end. Perhaps that is why a number of writers have recently been concerned to retell for the interested reader the tale of how it all began, with Johannes Gutenberg in Germany. Reading such books is certainly an enjoyable and informative occupation, but there is something unsatisfying about it for me, like reading a tale half told. To get back to the very beginning involves travelling back more than twice as far as to Gutenberg's Germany and to a time and place so different from our own that its way of life is still, for all the global widening of our horizons, largely unfamiliar, at any rate in the British Isles. For those who would seek them out, however, the connecting threads that link us across the miles and across the centuries are still there to be found.

Admittedly, it is necessary to go a very long way back, to an age that most people do not think about very often if at all. The best place in Britain to get a view of such remote times is not the Essex coast, but much further up in the far northwest, at Jarrow in Northumberland. It is here, in a sense, that the story of England itself begins, with the Venerable Bede in his monastery composing the first English history, relating how by accepting Christianity the Saxons became part of the wider civilised world of his day. If the clock were to turn back precisely thirteen hundred years, however, he would have been somewhat younger than the age at which he is generally depicted, and still not even on the point of starting his most famous work. Instead, he would have been found writing his commentary on the Book of Revelations, thinking of the future rather than the past, and not necessarily contemplating a comfortable future, either. The last book of the Bible would have seemed not an opaque allegory to him, but something pressing, something of immediate relevance. It is even conceivable that suspicions that the conversion of his people might simply be the prelude to the apocalyptic end of all human history might have made him hesitate to write about the process as history at all.

So if for a moment he raised his eyes and looked out across the sea, his gaze might well have been in the direction of Rome, where his hero, Pope Gregory the Great, had already foreseen one possible consequence of missionary activity as hastening the coming of the end. Gregory, as Bede records, had even sent letters warning his new English converts not to be surprised if the fate of mankind suddenly took a turn for the worse. No doubt, too, such thoughts, if they did enter Bede's mind, would have prompted him to gaze yet further in his imagination, to Byzantium, where an emperor still ruled, even though hard pressed by the turmoil that had engulfed the Middle East since the advent of Islam. That event had caused men to look yet further afield for possible allies in the uncertain times to come, far beyond their own world of the Mediterranean to the distant lands of Asia.

And men had come on embassies from those parts to Byzantium already – men whose homes were on the open steppes that stretched from horizon to horizon, with the result that what they had to say about those parts was carefully noted down by chroniclers. No doubt the information came as something of a surprise. For though in earlier times vague accounts had filtered back to the Roman Empire of a people they called the Seres, who provided them through the intermediary of a long trade route with the silk they prized so much, that had been long ago. Now, according to these nomad warriors, things at the other end of the earth had taken a new turn. They knew a land, far beyond the deserts and mountains where their own empire lay, that possessed mighty armies. Here, about a century before Bede's own lifetime, vast campaigns of conquest had created a great and unified nation, where tree-lined waterways linked cities of unimaginable size. This land was rich indeed, but what impressed the nomads particularly was the way its wealth was poured out on the creation of religious images, far larger and more numerous than anything the Byzantines could boast, for all their fervent devotion to Christianity.[1]

The likelihood is that Bede knew nothing of these travellers' tales, even at second hand. But if his gaze had been able to carry onwards, right across the steppes to the capital of that great empire, he might have beheld a sight to make him lay down his pen and parchment, lost in wonder. There, before his eyes, a monk or holy man – though not of his faith – would have been standing in front of a monarch more powerful and more terrible than any the Christian world could envisage. And yet if Bede had been able to look into the holy man's eyes he would have seen not fear, but a deep intelligence, a mind capable of simultaneously embracing both the immediate facts of the murderous world of court life and the whole vastness of time and space. Only recently have experts begun to appreciate that man's extraordinary genius, and to guess at some of the secrets that lay deep within his thoughts, hidden even from the penetrating eye of his ruler.

Strangely enough, scholars now have a very good idea of what was in the female monarch's mind, too, as she came towards the end of a long life. Knowing what she had to look back on, also, one might all the more appreciate seeing a smile of triumph play across her lips. How long had she dreamed of this day? Surely not as far back as her childhood, when she lost her father, nor to that day when the political connections he had built up paid off for her family and she was dispatched, barely a teenager, to the great imperial palace in the capital, to take her place amongst the emperor's many harem women. That emperor, the man responsible more than any other for pulling the country together, was already nearing the end of his reign, and though it is said she made an impression of sorts on him, by the time his strength was finally sapped by the great efforts he had made to set his dynasty on a stable base she was still no more than a lowly concubine, destined to mourn him for ever in the cold isolation of some closely guarded nunnery. Had her dreams already begun to take shape when, in a desperate gamble to elude that fate, she started an affair with the emperor's son? Probably not, but as she found herself against the odds installed as an imperial favourite of a much younger man, she must have realised the possibilities now open to her, and the steps she would have to take to keep her dreams alive. And what a life it had turned out to be, one that saw her rise from among those serried ranks of imperial women to become rather swiftly much more than the new emperor's indispensable helpmeet and companion, as he treated her as a co-regent, recognising her role as almost that of an equal. After his death, she had advanced, unlike any woman before or after her, yet further. She had ended up the ruler, not simply in fact but also in name, of the whole teeming empire that her husband had inherited. Sure enough, in the process she had made many enemies, and was prone to imagine many more. Yet she had always dealt with them with a ruthlessness that would have staggered her late husband from the start, had her remarkable beauty not completely blinded him to her faults, a beauty that had by no means faded, even now, in old age. This much no doubt Bede, had he really seen the two figures, would probably have been able to divine without much help, as a man already familiar with the ways of both power and faith.

Nothing in his experience, however, or even that of his successors, could have prepared him to comprehend the true extent of that woman's talents, or the enormity of her cruelty. A full description of her extraordinary life and times would tax the powers of the best narrative historian, since her life reads like the plot of some richly exotic novel, with the result that it has as often attracted the talents of historical novelists as of modern academics, let alone pious chroniclers equivalent to Bede.[2] Later Anglo-Saxon Britain did not lack for powerful and even murderous women – Elfryth, for example, stepmother and probable murderer of the unfortunate child-king Edward the Martyr. Further away, in Byzantium, the Empress Irene is remembered for having put out the eyes of her own son, the Emperor Constantine VI. In both cases isolated acts of wickedness have shaped their reputations. But here was a woman for whom ties of affection or kinship seemed to mean nothing whatsoever, and who caused death after death, apparently, as far as her contemporaries were concerned, without the least compunction. Two typical examples may give a flavour of her methods. In her widowhood she took a lover, a low-born, violently fanatical cult leader, who for a while seems to have served her political purposes as a sort of private chaplain, helping her acquire an aura of religious mystery. Once those purposes were served, however, she simply had him beaten to death.[3] Two daughters-in-law were likewise brutally murdered at her behest and unceremoniously buried in an unmarked grave as the result of false accusations, leaving her son too scared to protest, especially when two mandarins who visited him without his mother's permission were cut apart at the waist in a public execution.[4]

Some of the stories about the needlessly unpleasant deaths she inflicted on early rivals in the imperial harem, and the allegation that she poisoned her own son when he showed signs of opposing her, may be unreliable. But it is quite certain that from the beginning to the end of her long career many people died because of her. Only her ability to control her husband, and thereafter her extraordinary talents as a leader in her own right, kept her alive. For even those who hated her had to admire her qualities as a ruler. She had a particular gift for selecting the right officials, and took steps to improve their recruitment. Many, of course, were hired for their talents as informers and torturers, but she could also find the right men to keep international trade flowing and external enemies at bay. She particularly appreciated a talent for propaganda, and is said to have remarked of one brilliant young writer (who wrote a famously pungent manifesto for a group of unsuccessful rebels against her rule) that it was a pity that he was not on her team – though it is unlikely that this saved his skin.[5] It was no doubt as much to protect herself as for any other reason that she cultivated that aura of supernatural power, through the publicising of alleged prophecies, apparent miracles and, eventually more tangibly, through the creation of a series of grandiose public works so vast that to most of her subjects they must have seemed miraculous in themselves – a great obelisk, even larger religious images, and towering buildings, hundreds of feet tall. Had Bede seen such things, even with his knowledge of the splendours of Rome, he too would have been amazed.

But within the small-scale tableau I have imagined, what would have truly astonished him would have been something not immediately so noticeable, yet on closer observation the focus of the entire scene. For both faraway figures would have been concentrating on the slips of writing material that the holy man held in his hands. The material would have been unfamiliar to Bede, but he would probably have recognised it as akin to the papyrus that his predecessors in the Mediterranean world had employed before tougher times called for tougher books made of vellum. And strange as this stuff may have been, he would quickly have spotted something much stranger than the material itself. For not only were all of the dozens and dozens of slips that the holy man held up to show the woman identical in size. On each one there was writing, unfamiliar writing in a script that Bede might have guessed had something magical about it. And on every single slip – sheet after sheet after sheet – the writing, intricate as it was, was completely the same as on all the others, right down to the last dot. There were plainly too many sheets for even the most careful scribe to have copied out. What magic had created them? And why did the empress-turned-emperor smile so triumphantly when she saw them, as though she truly believed that her greatest wish were about to come true?

The scene is, of course, imaginary – though if Bede had had supernormal powers of vision, it could have happened. But the questions it raises were and are real ones, as much for us as they would have been for Bede. Most remarkably, too, scholars are able to answer them, if only in a provisional way. Thanks in no small part to the miraculous technology just described, it is now possible to do more than merely ponder the use of mute artefacts. We can try to understand the ways of thinking, even the individual motivations, of the historical personalities involved as well, on the basis of their surviving words. The one-time dwelling place of the Seres under the empress-emperor is as little known to most Europeans today as it was in Bede's time. But a quarter of mankind looks back to her age as a time when her nation was rightfully renowned and respected far and wide. Then, as has already been noted, her land was a magnet for traders across Asia and beyond, and a military power capable of enforcing the imperial will in regions far distant from her own capital. Even if they do not associate printing specifically with her name, they know that the beginnings of the technology most probably date back to her day, if not earlier.

To these people, then, the story of printing – amongst other stories – means something rather different from what it means to those parts of the world that approach history from a Eurocentric standpoint. This presents anyone writing in English with a difficulty, since one naturally expects a study of the origins of printing in English to so be about Gutenberg, so a book in which this name comes at the end of a process can only seem surprising – avoiding, as it were, the real, the proper origins of the technology. Important things happened in Europe at that time, certainly. But those of us who have been brought up within European traditions have for too long been used to thinking that important things – meaning things that affect us still today – only ever happened in Europe, with the result that what happened in the time of the Venerable Bede on the other side of the world has been overlooked. Even so, hundreds of millions of average readers of languages other than (for example) English actually think otherwise, and the descendants of the Seres, the Chinese of today, do not simply publish incessantly on the origins of printing in their country but also celebrate it in other ways: for instance in illustrations of early printing created by much the same methods used since those dim and distant times.[6] It is also worth pointing out that some historians are beginning to wonder whether the assumption that the only really important things happen in Europe might not be an unfortunate inheritance from a more blindly imperialistic age.[7]

One way to grasp the shift in outlook that is required is to consider a number of questions raised by the invention of printing by means of some analogies. There are three that it may be helpful to raise before getting down to telling our tale.[8] The first is this: 'Why is Rudolph C. C. Diesel (1858–1913) not considered the father of the railway locomotive?' Why don't historians write the history of the railways in the following way:

> The great German inventor Rudolph Diesel was the first man to provide a practical solution to the design of the independent railway locomotive. With the support of the innovative industrial firm of Krupps, who were generous patrons of research, he devised his revolutionary 'rational heat motor', based on compression ignition, in 1897. Before his time the prevailing locomotive technology was based on heating water with coal, a slow and messy technique that had first started on the periphery of Europe, where its first application was simply to move supplies of coal around. Though these rather primitive devices were eventually adapted to the transport of passengers, they completely lacked the many advantages of Diesel's invention, so that by the second half of the twentieth century these 'steam engines', as they were called, which required the constant presence of a 'fireman' on board shovelling coal into the device, were being rapidly driven out of use by the superior German technology even where they had been longest established.

For anyone brought up in Britain in the mid-twentieth century, though, the steam train for all its shortcomings is more likely to be a fond memory, even if the technology is scarcely used these days except by those who like a bit of nostalgia. Yet that is not the way many people tend to look at printing. Xylographic books, as experts term the sort of woodblock prints traditionally used in China, are seen by S. H. Steinberg in his standard account, *Five Hundred Years of Printing* as having 'outlived their usefulness' not long after they had been introduced, except as 'cheap tracts for the half-literate, . . . which anyway had to be very brief because of the laborious process of cutting the letters', a technology suitable only for products 'as disreputable as any modern horror comic'.[9] More recent writers might not perhaps write of popular culture in such terms, but even so the pointless effort required for xylography is still seen as its main distinguishing characteristic by as recent a work as John Man's *The Gutenberg Revolution*: 'wood-blocks were even more demanding than manuscript pages to make, and they wore out and broke, and then you had to carve another one – a whole page at a time'.[10] The simultaneous (or almost simultaneous) appearance of the block-book and of metal typography in Europe has reduced xylography to a mere episode, or even a footnote, in the history of the book for Westerners, and there has long been a tendency for Western writers to find something distinctly lacking in a culture like that of East Asia that found this apparently inferior technology perfectly acceptable for centuries. Discovering precisely how far back this attitude goes would take a fair amount of research, but amongst Europeans who knew at second hand of Chinese printing it is already quite evident in the eighteenth century.

At this early date, however, it was only Europeans who had never seen Chinese woodblock printing in action who tended to react in such a way; those who actually witnessed the production of books in China before the introduction of the latest, much improved forms of Western printing in the latter part of the nineteenth century reacted very differently. To the first Jesuit missionaries of the late sixteenth century, with their Counter-Reformation sensibilities, the cheapness and omnipresence of printing in China made the prevailing wood-based technology extremely disturbing, even dangerous. They much preferred the European situation, in which the higher start-up costs of metal-based printing – costs that had almost bankrupted Gutenberg – confined its use to a smaller circle of citizens of higher social standing, a group more amenable to the exercise of censorship.[11] By contrast, two hundred years later the Englishman John Barrow, who travelled on the 1793–5 Macartney mission to China, was generally quite dismissive of Chinese despotism, which accorded much less with his own temperament than it had done with that of the Jesuits, but even he had to confess with amazement that the press in China was 'as free as in England, and the profession of printing open to everyone'.[12] So, in short, while most people even today would be tempted to assume that the intricate Chinese writing system made printing difficult and hence of little consequence in China, those Western observers best placed to comment actually felt there was almost too much printing going on.

A little research into early nineteenth-century parallels between China and Britain further reveals that the comparative advantages of metal-based printing up to that point would appear to have been at the very least open to discussion. When the first Protestant missionaries were planning the introduction of the Bible into China, they took considerable pains to weigh up the advantages and disadvantages of various types of printing, and even communicated their results in a rather rare periodical published at the time in Canton. Though their initial use of woodblock was perhaps as much due to ready availability as any other advantage, they certainly did not regard the technology as hopelessly primitive. Despite Man's remarks, wooden blocks were often quite capable of being repaired or refurbished without too much effort, and, quite apart from initially advantageous start-up costs, they had the further economic advantage of making a book available by printing on demand for hundreds of years without it ever having to go 'out of print' and be

76   THIAN LŌ

"Lí ê chōe sī sià-bián." Tōe jī ê, kā i thǹg
phòa ê saⁿ, oaⁿ pēh ê saⁿ. Tōe saⁿ ê, ēng in,
in i ê thâu-hiàh; koh ēng chit kńg ê bûn-pin
hō͘ i, téng-bīn khàm-in; bēng-lēng i kiâ"lo
ê sī tch-khoaⁿ; nā kàu thiⁿ ê nńg thang
chiong chit kńg kau hō͘ i. Kóng soah, hi
Saⁿ Ê, ēng-kng ê chhàn-làn, chiù chòe in khi.
Hit sī Ki-tok tō put-chí hoaⁿ-hí, chài-saⁿ
phut-phut thiàu koh khì. Hit sī chiū gîm si,
　Kim koan sip kè pēng khong ēng,
　Chòe jîm tùⁿ khai ngó͘ tek seng;
　Chú tai û bòng sīn tēng ka,
　Ban liân lōk siōng Chú chí bēng.
堕空並架十觀令
生得我開䫫任罪
架釘身亡余代主
名之主頌樂年萬

LĖK THÊNG.   77

Hit sī Ki-tok tō kàu hia, chiǎ chhin-chhiū
si, kóng,
1 jú soat pēk chhú hô jîn?
Hoan kiàn kiù chéng sek hoàn sîn;
Î sī chòe hu bóng Chú gī,
Hoa mô͘ a chhàh piàu hoa sîn.
人何此白雪如衣
新換悉情應見翻
義主蒙夫罪是惟
身華表拚鴉毛華

Thian-lō lēk-thêng tōe it pún ê lō-bé.   芠

THE PERSISTENCE OF WOODBLOCK
1. A copy of *Pilgrim's Progress* in Romanised Hokkien from 1853, showing Western and Chinese block-cutter's pagination on the same page.

2. A woodblock from the late nineteenth century or later, made in Yunnan, from a monochrome image created from a photograph.

set up in type for a second edition.[13] Modern printing, of course is just as efficient in its way as Rudolph Diesel and the resultant diesel railway locomotive, but it was no more available at the start of the nineteenth century than Diesel's invention was to George Stephenson. The most recent survey of the arrival of modern printing in China, by Christopher A. Reed, shows how in their initial attempts at supplanting the traditional Chinese woodblock technology with more modern Western methods, missionary printers were obliged to try all sorts of drastic and expensive expedients, not excluding the time-consuming export of woodblocks back to New England to serve as the basis for stereotypes, which were then used to create publications for shipping all the way back to China.[14] Gutenberg letterpress printing based on the manual casting of fonts in fact never competed with woodblock: it was only the introduction of mechanical typecasting in the second half of the nineteenth century that eventually gave metal typography an advantage, though missionaries continued to use woodblock until many years later. Reed shows conclusively that the decisive breakthrough for China in terms of Western methods was not Gutenberg's letterpress, but lithography – a nineteenth-century technological breakthrough now almost forgotten in Europe.[15] And in any case, the all too common assumption that, because of supposed problems presented by the Chinese script, printing from woodblock in China before the introduction of Western technology can only have met aesthetic rather than commercial needs is, in the light of all the most recent research, plain wrong: books were cheap, even if they could have been cheaper, and they were most certainly easily obtainable.[16] Nor is this simply a deduction by contemporary scholars. Note in particular what one late nineteenth-century British observer had to say:

We have an extensive penny literature at home, but the English cottager cannot buy anything like the amount of printed matter for his penny that the Chinaman can for even less. A penny

Prayer-book, admittedly sold at a loss, cannot compete in mass of matter with many of the books to be bought for a few cash in China. When it is considered, too, that a block has been laboriously cut for each leaf, the cheapness of the result is truly marvellous and is only accounted for by the wideness of sale.[17]

The implications of this statement are plain enough. We should by no means underestimate the sheer commercial success of the Chinese technology, even when measured against nineteenth-century European standards.

So let us move on to another question. 'Why were the inventors of Meissen porcelain not as famous as Gutenberg?' After all, not everybody reads books even now, let alone over the past few centuries, but many more people use (or historically, by comparison with books, used) more basic items like cups and saucers. Not all have been able to afford the very best, but it is clear that the invention of porcelain in 1708 represented the dramatic achievement of an unsurpassable pinnacle in ceramic technology. And the story of how this was done is certainly extremely dramatic, especially when compared to what is known of Gutenberg's life – though even this seems to have had its ups and downs, which have allowed the British writer Blake Morrison, relying on existing historical research and a bit of imagination, to write it up as rather an impressive tale of struggle and somewhat qualified triumph.[18]

The story of Meissen porcelain, however, involved a boastful, alcoholic and conspicuously unsuccessful alchemist, Johann Friedrich Boettger (1682–1719), escaping from a failed attempt to transmute base metal into gold in Berlin for Frederick of Prussia only to end up in the employ of another autocratic ruler, the aptly named Augustus the Strong of Saxony (1670–1733), father of an alleged career total of over three hundred illegitimate children. Augustus needed money even more urgently than Frederick, though he was less interested in supporting his offspring than in spending on his other great passion, the acquisition of the very finest examples of porcelain imported from East Asia. When Boettger attempted another escape, and generally showed no signs of doing any better in Saxony than in Berlin, his employer put him under arrest and transferred him to another project that he was already supporting, namely the attempted creation of ceramics as translucent as the porcelain imports that were already draining the royal exchequer, and it was made perfectly clear to Boettger that failure in this further enterprise would incur the most severe royal displeasure. Though it is now known that for eventual success in this alternative enterprise the credit should not be assigned to Boettger alone – and some credit should surely go to Augustus for his creative research management techniques – the invention was considered at first important enough to be kept a state secret, and while that initial advantage was soon undermined by industrial espionage, the production of porcelain remained an important source of revenue to the area even when in the end it passed under Prussian control.[19]

Now the one simple fact that rather spoils the Meissen story is the prior discovery of porcelain in China, about a thousand years earlier. Though Boettger did not know how the manufacture of porcelain could be achieved, both he and Augustus can have been in no doubt that it was possible. But what did Gutenberg know about printing? In theory at least there were precedents available here too. I am, however, certainly not as impressed by the fact that the Koreans were printing with movable metal type in 1403 as are some recent scholars.[20] Technical difference aside, even earlier during the fourteenth century the trade routes across Asia to Europe were never as safe as some liked to believe, and by the end of that century the situation had become considerably worse, as John Larner points out in his fine study of Marco Polo, though it may be that the date of the Korean invention can be pushed back far enough to make transmission a little more likely.[21] I am much more impressed by the fact that even in England a limited form of metal typography, in the shape of the punches used and reused in the creation of coin dies, was routine in medieval times.[22] In any case the creation of the necessary moulds for producing type in quantity, and of the ink best suited to metal, and of the press itself, must be accredited to Gutenberg. Even if the specific creation of the hand-held type mould was a slightly later development, and the refinement of his ink may have owed something to advances in oil painting, his creative integration of several diverse elements into a single technology cannot be denied him. What puzzles me much more is the origin of the crucial idea of collecting types together in a frame to make up a page. As is acknowledged in the *Cambridge Medieval History*, Gutenberg was just one of a number of people striving towards the same goal.[23] How did they know it could be achieved? It is here that the history of the block-book gives us some interesting clues.

It has long been recognised that stylistic features in medieval European block-book illustrations point to influences from the East. The notion that this form of printing was not an independent invention, but came from Asia, is apparently still considered by experts to be quite unproblematic.[24] But T. H. Tsien, in his compendious standard account of Chinese printing, suggests that this importation was not just a matter of imitation, as in the case of porcelain: rather, certain features of woodblock carving technique common to East and West are identical in a way that cannot be accidental.[25] This would imply that the craft was taught, not imitated, either through a chain of intermediaries or directly, by a Chinese block-carver in Europe. The latter case is by no means as improbable as it sounds, since as I shall explain shortly the slave trade of the Mongol Empire, enthusiastically tapped by Italian traders, certainly did bring some East Asians to Italy.[26]

But can this be extended to include the introduction of a set of individual types in a frame? Surely no one from East Asia was in a position to teach that? I can see no reason why not. Movable type was probably arrived at as an option in China at quite an early point, especially since the refurbishment process in later times, and presumably almost from the start of printing, included the insertion of plugs bearing fresh individual characters wherever a wrong or defective character was detected in the original block – quite contrary to John Man's assumption that this form of printing required the start of a fresh block whenever an error was detected.

The term 'living' or 'movable block' was certainly already in use in the mid-eleventh century, when famously the first steps were taken to improve on movable wooden type by the introduction of a form of ceramic technology – something which later experiments have proved to be a perfectly feasible option, but which would probably have been too sophisticated for Europeans to emulate in any case, given how far behind they were in ceramic technology. For the most part, however, the whole-block approach remained the norm, as the Tangut term for movable type – which literally means 'broken-up characters' – indicates.

Now the Tanguts are scarcely remembered today, except perhaps as one of the many peoples whose kingdoms were obliterated by the armies of Genghis Khan. Indeed, the fact that it was the Tanguts who through their stiff resistance necessitated his final, fatal campaign – even though the great Mongol leader seems to have succumbed to disease rather than injury in battle – meant that they were subjected to a particularly brutal regime of massacre and enslavement. For Mongol success was built not simply upon terror and mass slaughter, but also on careful management of captured resources, with the result that in the course of Mongol expansion many craftsmen were spared and recruited into Mongol service. And in the days before Genghis Khan, when the Tanguts had dominated the trade routes entering China from the north-west, they had created a culture of great richness and individuality that clearly found employment for many craftsmen of Chinese origin. For their own writing system the Tanguts created a script at first glance similar to Chinese, though the characters, while regular enough in appearance, are actually on average appreciably more complex than in the true Chinese script, which was also used in their domains. This may have been deliberate: the Tanguts in effect could use the script as their own secret code, though there may also have been religious reasons for its adoption in a state that, thanks in part to its Tibetan neighbours, was suffused with belief in the mysteries of Tantric Buddhism.[27] In any case, the craftsmen in their employ did manage not only to bring woodblock art in the service of Buddhism to a very high level of artistic development, but also to perfect the techniques necessary for using movable wooden type.

Movable type, by no means a Chinese monopoly in East Asia, saw its greatest success in areas peripheral to China where other languages were used. Though these sometimes had their own scripts that (unlike Tangut) were less rather than more complex than Chinese, the fact that Chinese was still usually the earliest language to be printed in these areas suggests that a comparative lack of trained copyists or some other factor may have been at work unrelated to the relative difficulty or otherwise of a particular script for block or font carving.[28] Korea offers one such example: in that country movable metal type was used for the printing of books in Chinese script even before the distinctive Korean script was invented. This still makes Korea a possible source of inspiration for European printing, though there is no obvious route of transmission from there to Europe at the right time. In terms of possible westwards influence, therefore, attention amongst experts on East Asia has tended to concentrate on movable type in wood as used for Inner Asian languages, notably Uighur, for which the remains of a considerable wooden font were found at the start of the twentieth century. In Inner Asia wood was more scarce, and printing concentrated on Buddhist texts that kept to a fairly restricted religious vocabulary, perhaps limiting the font size required. The Buddhist scriptures were also plentiful enough not to require preservation on blocks to keep them available for circulation, so the incentives to manufacture reusable type, despite the considerable degree of woodworking skill required, were perhaps higher than elsewhere. The Uighurs, who lived somewhat further west than the Tanguts, though originally nomads, had developed over a period of living in the oases along the trade routes of Inner Asia a sophisticated civilisation based on trade and agriculture. The early absorption of their territories into Genghis Khan's conquests gave their new rulers the beginnings of a literate civil service, since the Uighurs were already using a script for their own language that was ultimately of alphabetic derivation.

Because the Uighurs, as the ubiquitous chief clerks of the Mongol empire, at that time maintained widespread links between East Asia and Europe, they might naturally be seen as the most likely intermediaries responsible for introducing typography to the West. This possibility has recently been strengthened by two discoveries. First, it now appears possible that at the start of the fourteenth century the Uighurs were attempting to print, on the main trade route from Inner Asia into China, a version of the Buddhist canon in their own language, an enterprise large enough to be noticed by passing traders. Second, directly contrary to earlier reports that they simply mimicked slavishly Chinese character-based typography by printing whole words, it has been shown that they neither did this nor printed in accordance with the underlying alphabetic nature of their script. Rather, they carefully adapted the use of movable type quite ingeniously to a middle course between these two options, in order to suit the particular features of their language. Typographers intelligent enough to do this would have had no trouble communicating their technology to Westerners.

Mongols, however, tended to try to keep a monopoly over any useful technology, though their position as monopolists was eroded somewhat by their progressive inability to act as one group, as the frequent open warfare between the Mongol Ilkhans of Persia and the Golden Horde of Russia from the late thirteenth century onwards demonstrates. Such internecine warfare in Asia during this period seems to have brought on to the well-known slave markets of the Black Sea, amongst constant fresh supplies for Italian traders, a group of captives originally from north-east of Tibet. For, as was long ago realised by at least one historian of technology, we suddenly see devices, until then typical of that cultural area, appearing on the open plains of Italy for no immediately visible reason.[29] To be precise, these new imports must have been craftsmen (no doubt partly or wholly of Chinese origin) from the Tangut area – and the Tanguts, as already mentioned, used movable wooden type, although this fact, first discovered in the 1930s, has tended until recently to be very seldom discussed. There are at least ten surviving examples of materials produced by Tangut movable type, going back well into the twelfth century. And since the Tanguts definitely did print a Buddhist canon in their language in China at the start of the fourteenth century, it is quite certain that their woodworkers maintained their fine carving skills even after their conquest by the Mongols.[30]

Using movable wooden type is certainly not easy, but it was plainly seen for a long time in East Asia as a viable option: the Japanese for example used this method to produce their Tenkai edition of the entire Buddhist canon in the early seventeenth century. But it does take a very high level of woodworking skill, and recently intriguing evidence has been examined suggesting that even if Tangut craftsmen had been able to demonstrate the technique in Europe, few Europeans would have been able to imitate them. In the eighteenth century the pioneer Sinologist Etienne Fourmont undertook the production of a Chinese font in wood, sponsored by the Regent of France. Though the font was quite large and clumsy by Chinese standards, it still took twenty years, many craftsmen and a massive investment of royal funding in order to reach completion.[31] For craftsmen working in the early fifteenth century without the benefits of the patronage of a large early modern absolutist monarchy to support them, the lesson from the East might well have been that it could be done, but they had to work out their own way to do it. That is just a hypothesis, of course, but it does draw Mainz and Meissen much closer together than admirers of Gutenberg usually care to acknowledge. At the very least, I do not think it is possible to be so certain of the mid-twentieth-century dictum that 'From the point of view of its effects on history, printing as it was done in China was sterile'.[32] That is simply not the only way in which the available evidence can now be construed.

The third introductory question that has to be considered is by contrast not directly concerned with the position of Europe in relation to the rest of the world, but with another assumption that tends to be made as a result of the European experience. Because stories such as that of Galileo being forced to repudiate his own scientific findings for religious reasons have become very widely familiar in the course of the rise of European science, there is a tendency to see religious forces as opposed to progress. But if at times there may have been some truth in this, it is necessary to be careful not to assume that technological change attracted similar religious opposition – surely there would have been no great medieval cathedrals without a willingness to introduce new building techniques. In particular we should probably be careful about assuming religious opposition to progress in a very different cultural situation. The question, then, is simply this: 'How did Gutenberg's printing of indulgences advance the cause of learning in the slightest?' That Gutenberg was involved not simply in the noble cause of multiplying Bibles and Latin grammars but also in the propagation of these cash certificates for the remission of sins and other less edifying forms of religious literature (publications more reminiscent of the ideas of apocalyptic cultists than of what one might prefer to imagine was mainstream biblical scholarship) is something that any balanced account of his work is obliged to mention – although somehow many manage to leave it out.[33] Even these activities may of course be seen as pushing forward the course of history: in Barbara Tuchman's phrase, indulgences were the 'seed of the Reformation', so the innovation of printing may perhaps be construed as no more than the invention of a seed drill, ensuring a more bountiful harvest.[34] But it should not be concluded that Gutenberg himself was like some liberal eighteenth-century British squire, keen to improve the world in which he found himself. Blake Morrison, for example, allows himself a little flight of fantasy in which Gutenberg, inspired by some doves taking grain from his hands, envisions the book of the future, liberated from the slowness of scribes: just as a dove opens its wings and flies away with the seed it has taken from his hand, so may books now open their pages and fly forth much more rapidly with the seed of knowledge.[35]

In what is otherwise an enjoyable and generally (as far as I can tell) very accurate evocation of Gutenberg's world, this passage comes across as introducing an entirely false, post-Renaissance note. It is not simply that what the man himself and his earliest rivals created was at first no more than a greater volume of purely medieval reading matter, even if soon enough new forms of knowledge came to the fore.[36] One should not forget either that Gutenberg's first get rich quick scheme was nothing to do with learning of any sort at all: it was a venture in the manufacture of small portable convex mirrors, which pilgrims could use like periscopes to look over the shoulders of thronging crowds of devotees to catch a glimpse of a holy relic. John Man, again reflecting a more modern point of view, introduces this story as a 'small detour to the wilder shores of religious eccentricity'.[37] By early fifteenth-century standards – and most certainly by fourteenth-century standards, with its plagues, pogroms, penitent flagellants and prophecies of doom – this was surely completely normal, mainstream activity, an activity that Gutenberg seems to have no qualms about responding to. After all, so desperate were the crowds of the age for a little reassuring contact with the holy that in the wicked world in which they found themselves technology was arguably better addressed to catering to their terrible spiritual hunger than to deluging them with copies of Cicero and other worthy classical authors.

This may all seem entirely obvious. But the temptation to read history as a tale of successive technological triumphs bringing better and better things is a remarkably insidious one. It has even been seen as infecting Elizabeth Eisenstein's well-known and deservedly influential work on printing, which has brought home to us just how deep and rapid the impact of Gutenberg's invention was in Europe – though she also gives full credit to the simultaneous influence of woodblock printing, whose technical potential (including the potential for the repair and upgrading of blocks) she certainly does not underrate.[38] It must be conceded, however, that by examining Europe in isolation she does not really have to grapple with the problem of how the market may or may not have affected the advance of the new technology. This factor only emerges as important when the spread of printing is considered comparatively, and it is no accident that the clearest vantage point from which to comment on the possible constraints imposed by a lack of readership has been the case of Japan, where it appears that printing was available for almost a millennium before it had any detectable popular impact.[39] Might the lack of a market explain why the invention of printing in East Asia, by contrast with Europe, seems to have had no apparent consequences, or at least an impact delayed for so very long?

This additional question is, strictly speaking, not one that falls within the scope of a book on the beginnings of printing, since it relates rather to the history of its exploitation, though the use in East Asia of non-alphabetic scripts seems largely irrelevant in light of the evidence cited above concerning the confrontation of Chinese and European techniques in the missionary printing of the nineteenth century. And when considering the spread of printing in China one wonders if the lack of impact is more apparent than real. In a world already very well supplied with manuscript materials written not on parchment but on the cheap and universally available medium of paper, the transition to a world in which printed material, though it may have taken on in places a more dominant role, also continued to use paper cannot have been as immediately obvious. If there is an answer to the question, it probably lies in large part in the later centuries of Chinese history, not as far back as the time of Bede but in the very different society that had already begun to emerge there before Anglo-Saxon Britain was transformed by the Normans. Treating that whole story, dynasty after dynasty, would make for a narrative of much more epic proportions, though tracing the development of printing in China for a few centuries from the time of its first use in imperial circles does point to some intriguing possibilities. Fortunately, other researchers are currently engaged in exploring the later phases of Chinese printing, so a few centuries may suffice for this study of origins.[40]

For the moment, though, one final point that needs to be made is that any assumption that the development of printing in China actually had no consequences even for East Asia, let alone the world, bears very strong echoes of the 'Needham Question' in the history of science, another celebrated attempt at discovering why against all reasonable expectations 'nothing happened' in China.[41] This was the question that initially struck the great historian of science, Joseph Needham (1900–93), when he started to learn about the Chinese traditions in his field. Why was it that, with all its immense premodern achievements, China had not been the country in which modern science had appeared? Needham was some way into a distinguished career when this thought first occurred to him, and after spending some time in China during the Second World War it came to dominate the rest of his long life, leading eventually to the creation in Cambridge of the Needham Research Institute where, beyond a doorway and past a statue of its founder, research still continues. For the 'Needham Question' has now outlived its author. Indeed, in addressing its original query, he and his immediate associates and successors have so far published almost a couple of dozen stout volumes of investigations into many aspects of Chinese science and technology. Even more studies have been produced in response by other researchers. This at least suggests that not all big questions can be dismissed in short answers. One can see that the fact that printing existed in China from about the same time as porcelain, but – as in Japan, too – with the apparent lack of the effects documented for Europe by Eisenstein, does pose a question, or quite possibly a part of the same 'Needham Question', too. And perhaps what is even more baffling is an alternative way of looking at the same problem, that is: how come, if China was as useless in exploiting this technology as Japan, it was invented there in the first place?

Pointing out these apparent anomalies just goes to show that by simply touching upon a puzzle it is all too easy to trigger a whole series of new questions. That is why rather than pursue all the issues raised by Chinese printing at once, it is probably more sensible to go back and consider what has come out of the answers to the first three questions that have already been asked. First, from asking about Diesel and his engine it is possible to conclude that we cannot simply transpose our own narratives about our technologies, about our own heroes like Gutenberg and his successors, into other contexts and expect them to explain very much. We run the risk thereby of ignoring examples of important technologies such as the steam engine just because they were eventually replaced. Second, by comparing the inventions of porcelain and printing we learn that this does not mean that different contexts need be considered as existing, as it were, in parallel universes, entirely without any influence on one another. The mere possibility of an awareness in Europe before Gutenberg of some features of Chinese printing makes it well worth knowing about in terms of our own history. Third, when we look at the religious world of Gutenberg's day we can see that the reasons for the emergence of new technologies must be sought against a background of the demands of the age in which they were introduced, not in relation to their uses in later times, even if it takes us some effort of imagination to grasp what those original demands were. This last principle, in fact, might be applied more widely than with regard to the religious environment alone. The whole historical situation that gave rise to printing needs to be understood in terms of the way things looked at the time, not how they look today – that is really what the work of the historian is all about. For example, in the case of China it will be necessary to come up with an account of the origins of printing that does not assume that it was intended to supply more books, since, as the reader will find out, the Chinese were very well supplied with books in any case. The bigger questions, like that raised by Needham, comparing longer-term consequences in East and West are, of course, important as well, but one would hope that a careful account of the origins of Chinese printing might allow us to refine them, to ask those bigger questions in a form more relevant to the actual situation that a reading of the sources reveals.

This means that the account that follows here of necessity starts quite a long time ago – further back than the main focus of this book in the centuries around about the time of Bede, and far back enough to give some account of the deeper cultural background that eventually gave rise to printing. And even that is not enough. For as well as trying to deduce the latent possibilities for the invention of printing hidden within the cultural matrix of the original civilisation of early China, it is also necessary to go on to give some account of another civilisation, too: that of India. The holy man contemporary with Bede whom I have brought into his imaginary vision of events in China was, in fact, a Buddhist monk, and partly non-Chinese at that, while his ruler herself had at one time apparently been a Buddhist nun. Without some account of the Buddhist religion, and one or two of the key notions with regard to technology and especially to the religious role of replication that it introduced to China from India, no analysis of the view from Jarrow will make any sense. After these preliminaries, the story of the emergence of printing is one of putting together all the clues it is possible to find in sources that – for reasons that are on reflection quite understandable – are not very interested in telling us much about its invention or use. Within that sequence of clues, however, the story of the priest and the empress does deserve special treatment, since the circumstantial evidence would appear to show that it marked a new phase in the use and spread of the technology. Even for a couple of centuries after this point the clues to the spread of printing are still somewhat meagre, but in view of the puzzle about its impact, they too are surely worth pursuing. And once all the evidence has been outlined, we can come back to the bigger issues raised here, with a better appreciation of how it all began – possibly even an appreciation of what it might all mean, or possibly, as Joseph Needham eventually found out, with a clearer idea of how many books it might take to get something like a proper answer.

In the pages that follow, therefore, no attempt has been made to produce a comprehensive survey of all the issues surrounding the appearance and adoption of printing in China. That remains a task for the future. The aim is to open up the topic for other historians by looking at those aspects of the story that have been ignored so far, chiefly those relating to religion and ideology. The researchers most likely to add to our knowledge are the archaeologists, but one can never predict what will turn up: much of our account of the psychology of the woman ruler that explains her possible interest in printing stems from a completely chance discovery made a few years ago. Yet in order to interpret any future evidence scholars will need to be aware of the ideas of the age, not just of the material culture, or even of the extraordinary personalities who stamped their individuality on the age. The study of the rise of printing is a study of the way women and men were thinking, just as much as it is a study of the technologies they invented. But of course one does not have to go as far as China to discover that.

CHAPTER TWO

A MESSAGE FROM IRAKLION

To see the oldest printed document in the world, it is necessary to travel to a museum in Europe, but not one of the better-known ones. The museum of Iraklion, on the Greek island of Crete, houses a clay disc, recovered in 1908 from the ancient site of the city of Phaistos, on which forty-five different symbols have been stamped in a sequence of 242 characters over its two sides.[1] No one knows what the characters mean, or even where the disc was made, since nothing similar has been discovered on the island. It seems likely that it dates to about 1500–1200 BCE, and that the stamp for each symbol was made of gold. Whoever invented this technique would only have needed to set the individual stamps in a frame so that they could have made an imprint onto a piece of soft clay all at once, and whatever message this strange writing conveys could have been reproduced many times without much effort. So close did the Mediterranean world come to anticipating Gutenberg. But the message from Iraklion is that nobody ever did, because nobody ever wanted to.

It is easy to see that the invention of this set of types could have evolved quite naturally from the use of seals in the ancient world.[2] It is equally easy to see that using this method of printing on to clay by hand would have been a bit like using a disassembled typewriter to type on paper: under most circumstances, it would be quicker simply to write in longhand. Certainly, after the introduction of papyrus, the reed pen and 'cursive' scripts, usually based on a simplified writing system such as the Roman alphabet, the individual character stamp as a means of writing a message would have seemed very slow indeed. In China writing cannot be traced back any earlier than to the time of the Phaistos disc, and until the invention of paper fifteen hundred years later the main writing materials were bamboo slips, which were rather bulky for extensive, book-length writing, or silk, which was expensive. But researchers have discovered that from as early as it is possible to trace the use of writing, the Chinese were already using the brush to form characters, even if according to legend the invention of the brush came much later, and this would have made freehand writing extremely quick.[3] Indeed, once paper had been invented, the speed of writing then possible in conjunction with the extreme concision of Chinese in its classical literary form apparently made court reporters unnecessary, since any educated clerk could perform the task of accurately noting down the contents of speech at speed.[4]

A study of our main source on written materials during the age of paper, the 40,000 manuscripts and fragments from a surviving monastic library at Dunhuang in China's north-west, sealed about a thousand years ago, tends to suggest that such speedwriting was not just a recent phenomenon.[5] In early China this was not generally the case: some writing – including almost all that survives – was created quite laboriously on intractable surfaces, sometimes even where it could not be read. Placing writing on the inside of ritual vessels might seem strange, but it should be borne in mind that it was not only men who could read: the all-seeing inhabitants of the invisible spirit world were also familiar with writing.[6] One later account of the origins of writing stated that it was the great secret originally known only to the spirits – just as in ancient Greece fire was the secret of the gods stolen by Prometheus for the benefit of mankind – and that when mankind caught up with them by inventing writing, the sound of spirits lamenting this loss of their monopoly was heard in the night. This phenomenon the second-century CE commentator explains by saying that the spirits were afraid that mankind would now be enabled to put spells on them.[7] The First Emperor, Qin Shihuangdi (ruled 221–210 BCE), unifier of China and lord of the famous terracotta warriors, carved inscriptions on China's mountains telling of his achievements, but it was the gods that he was addressing just as much as his subjects; indeed, by introducing a new, regularised version of the Chinese script himself he was assuming a divine role.[8] The aura of the supernatural that surrounds the Chinese written word is not entirely unique to Chinese civilisation. We speakers of English should recall that our own word 'glamorous', whatever it may mean now, originally meant 'magical, supernatural', and derives from the notion of 'grammar' or the knowledge of writing as something arcane and mysterious.[9] But the more that is discovered about this period that experts call 'Early China', the more it becomes clear that writing, whatever other purposes it served, was deeply embedded in a world of ritual practices that are only just beginning to be understood.[10]

Yet these supernatural associations did not preclude the completely pragmatic use of writing by the First Emperor in running his empire. As well as his warriors, he employed serried ranks of administrators to create an empire based on the written word in which efficiency was the keynote. All the copying and communication within his empire these men could carry out quite effectively by using their brushes. The records of routine documents recovered from a slightly later period show for example that site inspection reports from China's northern borders recorded even quite trivial points, like the state of the guard dog kennels. In other words, this was not a society that found the routine use of writing for record keeping or communicating a problem.

On one point, however, the First Emperor did wish to address all his subjects as directly as possible, and that was on the very essence of his achievement: his unification of the norms by which people had lived according to separate standards in different states before his time – their weights and measures. Since setting unified standards lay at the heart of his conception of government, he composed a short text of forty Chinese characters vaunting his decree on this topic. This may be found reproduced on a number of bronze and ceramic measuring vessels, even if ironically enough neither the forms of the (supposedly equally standardised) characters used in the message nor even the weights and measures that the imperial message purports to guarantee are quite as standardised as he had decreed.[11] Perhaps because he became aware of the former discrepancies, on some of these the text has been split into ten groups of blocks of four characters each, applied to these vessels during their manufacture.[12] This was not exactly a breakthrough in terms of the principles involved: characters had been transferred to bronzes (though on a 'one-off' basis) by similar techniques centuries earlier, while the use of seals, and of pattern blocks applied to textiles, was quite common by this time. The underlying idea of 'modularising' the text runs very deep in the Chinese approach to organising production, that is, breaking down complex elements of any design into subsidiary units: one only has to think of the First Emperor's terracotta army as a brilliant exploitation of this method of manufacture.

In this case the vast variety of Chinese characters all have the status of signs of equal size, for all of them – whether complex or simple, symmetrical or apparently lop-sided – fit into rectangles of identical size that can be arranged in a grid pattern.[13] In fact the notion of circulating brief messages created by means other than handwriting was in a sense not new by this point, either in China or in the Mediterranean world, since the coinage that had been introduced in both areas carried written inscriptions, even if only of a handful of words at the most.

Yet the First Emperor's willingness to use a form of printing in this particular case, even a sort of forerunner of movable type printing, prompts the speculation that if he had had more tractable materials available, such as paper, he might have gone on to address his subjects through mass printing on other topics also. But this supposition may owe too much to our own contemporary notions of cost efficiency in communication, and may not take account of contemporary views of the matter. Although in the earliest phase of Chinese writing the brush was already available, much of what survives today was laboriously created in other media – incisions in bone or shell, and writing formed on cast metal. Notions of prestige and permanence plainly played a part in 'public' writing, whether addressed to humans or gods, and it would seem that inscriptions on metal or stone had a certain status above that of everyday writing on wood. Mastery in this area, as with the First Emperor's inscriptions on the mountains, demonstrated imperial power. His own dynasty was famously short-lived, scarcely surviving beyond his own death, and it was his eventual successors, the rulers of the Han dynasty (202 BCE–CE 220), who put the Chinese imperial system on a firm footing. Yet even they began to lose their grip on power after three centuries of rule, and it is interesting to see what measures they took to bolster their prestige. As guardians of the written heritage of earlier times, the dynasty decided to carve on to stone tablets all the texts associated with the great sage Confucius: six ancient works which he was supposed to have edited for posterity plus the *Analects of Confucius* containing his own sayings. This amounted to slightly over 200,000 Chinese characters, whereas in the contemporary Mediterranean world an inscription even of 25,000 words was considered extraordinary.[14] Techniques for creating inscriptions do not seem to have been dissimilar, so rather than look to technology to explain this difference, we should look to the role of the imperial state with regard to writing in China – the Western inscription in question, covering all the works of an Epicurean philosopher in Greek, was created not by the state, but by a private citizen.

By the time the task of engraving this huge amount of Chinese text on stone had been completed in CE 183, paper had been officially known at court for some time, since its 'invention' is dated to 105, though there is archaeological evidence of its use as a wrapping material rather earlier than this, as well as various indications of its earlier function as a writing material. To have used it to make a copy of the 'Confucian Canon' would have involved no prestige at all, so no one has any idea when the transfer of these materials to paper first took place, since no one saw fit to mention it – even though the inscribing of the same materials onto stone was treated as a major event. It is a lucky chance that the date of CE 105 was recorded, because Cai Lun, the official involved, who seems to have introduced some improvement in paper manufacture, worked at the palace as a eunuch. Yet just because the new technology was not trumpeted at the time does not mean that it had no effect. On the contrary: up to this point China was lagging behind those Mediterranean societies where papyrus was used and where light, inexpensive scrolls could be created. But thereafter the advantage swung the other way, since papyrus, which is composed of organic material not as highly processed as paper, was prone to splitting and deterioration at a much greater rate; this may be why vellum eventually came to dominate, especially in the harsher climate of Northern Europe. Paper, by contrast, gave a good, uniform writing surface that could be smoothly rolled and unrolled without damage, while remaining relatively durable.

It is in fact quite hard to think of printing without paper. Gutenberg did print one of his Bibles on vellum, but his run of thirty-five copies is calculated to have entailed the slaughter of five thousand head of cattle, so one can imagine the carnage required if this was the only material available to support the nascent printing industry in Europe, let alone what would be needed for hard copy today.[15] At least this formed some sort of improvement on the great age of illuminated manuscripts, when a single Bible could have accounted for some five hundred calves.[16] The sort of situation implied by Gutenberg's work would have entirely prevented not simply the rise of printing but also the administration of the Chinese empire during the age of Bede thirteen centuries ago. It is not just that, shortly after Bede's lifetime in England, the taxation system in China would appear to have required for a population not much smaller than that of France or Italy today the production of tens of thousands of population registration files annually in the imperial local administrative system alone. When one factors in provincial and central records, a total of a quarter of a million administrative files created annually looks quite likely.[17] Any production of animal skins processed as writing materials even at a fraction of the rate required would probably have been very strongly resisted, since by that time Buddhist influence in China was at its apogee, and a strong current of vegetarianism and concern for the preservation of animal life meant that many would have scrupled not at the economic cost but at the spiritual cost in terms of bad karma.

By that time China had changed radically since the days of the First Emperor or even since the later stages of the Han dynasty. It had gone through a process of disintegration and collapse similar in some respects to the decline and fall of Rome, and perhaps some common factors were at work, such as a lengthy period of environmental change towards a colder climate, with accompanying famine, and disease in the wake of famine. Improved long-distance communications during the Han dynasty resulted in the rise of Buddhism in China at about the same time that Christianity was beginning to make its mark on Europe. But the existence of paper in China means that it would be unwise to take these analogies to imply a roughly similar course in the transition from Antiquity to the Middle Ages. In Europe that transition has always been built around a sense of loss, the copious and vibrant literature of ancient times suffering a slow attrition that even the Renaissance was unable to reverse, since so much had disappeared irretrievably before multiple copies could be made by printing. Certainly much of the early literature of China from before imperial times was lost – and not just because the First Emperor is said to have taken steps to burn much of it in a grandiose attempt to censor historical memory of life before his own times, but because of what one might term 'natural causes' also. The use of bamboo and silk, however, made written materials buried earlier rather more readily retrievable – Chinese history records one case in CE 281, though this is somewhat unusual and only modern archaeology has added substantially to our stock of written materials from this period.[18] No doubt the contemporary world is still missing much that might once have provided a more intelligible reflection of Han times than it now possesses. Even so, it does not seem that literary production during this period ever reached the rates that the papyrus-based culture of the Mediterranean was able to achieve. No event like the burning of the library at Alexandria ever took place, because no Chinese library at this point came close to it in size.

Paper arrived at just the right time to start a process of literary accumulation that not only saw the Chinese written heritage through some very rough patches but also allowed it to increase in size at a steady rate. A strong reading culture seems to have developed quickly after its introduction, despite political fragmentation. The first silent reader to appear in Chinese sources, some time before St Ambrose in the West, is Ruan Dan (CE 281–310), and thereafter even though recitation remained dominant as an educational tool, silent reading seems to have been a recognised option into the age of print.[19] Ruan himself lived through grim times, but did not see the worst that was to befall. The collapse of the Han dynasty in rebellion and bloodshed was followed in the third century CE by a three-way struggle between warlords that was to see the winner's dynasty rapidly supplanted by a regime so fratricidal that its efforts at tearing itself apart in the early fourth century were just as rapidly overtaken by a great uprising of non-Chinese warriors in north China. For just as the Romans had brought within their frontiers 'barbarian' troops to keep out even more barbarous peoples beyond the empire, so the ethnic picture in north China had become complicated by similar expedients. Now, however, in 312 the immigrants had had enough of seeing the Chinese squabbling among themselves. The capital was sacked, forcing many of its inhabitants to flee south to the valley of the Yangzi, where a refugee remnant of the dynasty was able to perpetuate a Chinese rule that was to endure, despite several subsequent changes of regime. Thus China fell apart much more rapidly than the Roman Empire into halves, and one of the halves from the start was under alien leadership of a profoundly unstable type, as various groups of warriors of non-Chinese origin attempted to establish order out of chaos. The attendant looting and burning undoubtedly accounted for the destruction of a great deal of early literature. But paper was certainly well established by the late third century, so that whatever the destruction, diligent copying seems to have made good at least some of the losses; even in the north habits of scholarship do not seem to have become entirely extinct, as the warrior regimes more often than not found themselves obliged to rely on Chinese bureaucrats to organise a taxation system more lucrative in the long run than sporadic raiding. Of course southerners were not always very impressed by levels of learning in the north. One southern general who temporarily reconquered a northern capital in the early fifth century found a mere four thousand old scrolls in the palace library – the sort of collection that could be built up by an ordinary private citizen in the south.[20] Emperors there were not beyond bestowing thousands of scrolls on individual courtiers simply as gifts.[21] In time, however, a certain degree of stability in the north during the fifth century allowed for some catching up to take place. Early in the sixth century it is possible to point to individual scholars in both north and south capable of citing more than four hundred sources in commenting on earlier works.[22] By contrast, two centuries later in England, the Venerable Bede, who had at his disposal the best library north of the Alps, was familiar only with about three hundred books.[23] An individual in China with access to an imperial library by this stage could probably read much more widely. Although unfortunately two great encyclopaedias compiled in north and south during the sixth century have been lost, it has been established that one smaller compilation of the seventh century cites over 1,400 works – though I suspect that many of them are second-hand quotations based on entries already excerpted in one of these larger predecessors.[24]

In some respects, it is not these pinnacles of scholarship that impress so much as the stray asides of scholars throwing light on the extraordinary availability of written materials in China by the middle of the first millennium. Doubtless the image we have of scribes in Europe at this time toiling painfully slowly through page after page of manuscript, quill in hand, partakes of a picture of monkish restrictions on learning that make the liberating role of Gutenberg that much more impressive. But when the sources reveal that one Chinese scholar made it his practice to copy out fifty sheets of two hundred characters every day, it becomes quite clear how it was possible for individuals to build up a considerable collection by their own efforts without recourse to the book trade, which also seems to have existed since Han times.[25] This explains why even those scholars who pleaded poverty (even if, like Karl Marx, they seem to have had servants) do not appear to have experienced any difficulty in getting hold of books, even quite unusual ones. At the other end of the scale it is equally revealing to find a much richer figure uneasy about the number of books he had obtained in a not quite ethical way – presumably borrowed and not returned – putting the quantity of such material in his library in the region of 'at least two hundred scrolls'.[26] This contrasts intriguingly with some sage words of advice to his family offered by another scholar who lived through the very worst of this period, the climactic warfare of the late sixth century that, after a relative lull in hostilities at the beginning of the century, swept China towards a dramatic reunification. This man had in his time served as an imperial librarian in the south. But he had also been captured by enemies and enslaved twice, in the course of an eventful life that finally saw him end his days as a respected scholar far from the land of his birth in north China. His estimate is that possession of a few hundred scrolls, diligently studied, was all that was needed to ensure one's social standing as an educated man – and despite having himself hit rock bottom on more than one occasion, he did not consider a library of this size beyond the possession of any educated individual.[27]

The trick, of course, was to be born into a family that already possessed that quantity of books, so as to gain an education sufficient to make any soldier, however barbarous, think twice about killing you; not that one can presume that this always worked. Members of this group were a very small minority in the predominantly agrarian society of China during these centuries, but ever since the collapse of the Han dynasty they had developed, in the face of rulers of very uncertain quality, a distinct culture of their own, based on literary communication, a self-conscious shared participation in a cultural tradition.[28] At the heart of that tradition was an interlinked trio of expressive arts – poetry, painting and calligraphy – to which paper was central; in the case of the last-named art, paper was far more profoundly esteemed in East Asia than in lands using alphabetic scripts for it was essential. It was paper that gave the smooth, unlimited surface – a surface cheaper to obtain in quantity than silk – that made truly dynamic styles of calligraphic brushwork possible. The presumption was that, however benighted the world became, there would always be those prepared to preserve your calligraphy, imitate your painting, or copy out your poem, so that one day what you expressed of yourself would be recognised.[29] In later times paper, the brush, the ink and the inkstone used to prepare ink constituted the 'Four Treasures of the Scholar's Studio', the simple but much-esteemed accoutrements that made the high cultural tradition invulnerable to everything from Mongol invasion to the rise of popular culture up to the twentieth century. The tradition is by no means extinguished even yet.

Looking back at the contribution of paper not simply to China but to the development of human civilisation as a whole one cannot help feeling that it has been vastly underrated. Perhaps if we in the West had had the name of some European inventor of paper that we could celebrate in the same way that Gutenberg and other European claimants to his invention have been celebrated over the years we would all take paper much more seriously. The meticulous and widespread use of bookkeeping, for example, which has been important in Europe's rise to prosperity even if it is not its sole explanation, did not benefit at all from printing, but did require large quantities of paper for making manuscript records – much more material than could be supplied by vellum, at any rate.[30] Until very recently manuscript records, either unique or made in just one or two copies, have been essential not simply to Dickensian law offices but to the running of any large organisation, while even today electronic records on computers are not quite as problem-free as one might wish. Many libraries, for example, still distrust their cataloguing systems enough to hesitate to throw away their filing cards.

Given that in China from the third century CE onwards the intellectual leaders of the society found paper a particularly suitable cultural medium for asserting their individual and collective identities, it might even be possible to argue that the very strength of a paper- and brush-based information technology made the invention of printing less, not more, likely. Certainly some parts of East Asia have got by until modern times with very little in the way of printing, on the basis of a strong manuscript culture.[31] But the interplay of technology and society is not a simple matter. The message from Iraklion, whatever the literal meaning of the Phaistos disc, is that a technology can even be entirely forgotten if events take another turn. And by the time of the reunification of China in 589, the culture of East Asia had already taken a very different turn from that of the First Emperor's epoch and of the Han dynasty, though sometimes this is rather hard to tell from the writings of the intellectuals whose collections of scrolls were discussed above. Like some early Christian intellectuals in the West so steeped in the traditions of Antiquity that no hint of their personal beliefs can be discerned through their prose – the philosopher Boethius (*c.* 480–524) particularly comes to mind – Chinese scholars were generally such thoroughgoing classicists that any hint of an awareness of alien traditions of thought is equally hard to find. But many of them were believers in a religion of foreign origin too, in this case the religion of Buddhism. And the story of how printing came into being – though it involves Chinese religion, too, which requires its own explanation – cannot be told without understanding some very basic Buddhist practices and concepts. What the Buddha taught and, even more, how he taught it and what the consequences were for his disciples, are just as much part of the background to printing as the First Emperor and his measuring vessels. Once again it is necessary to leave China, this time for ancient India.

CHAPTER THREE

THE BUDDHA'S WORD

Mankind today can look back on the Buddha, the 'Enlightened One', as one of the most successful religious teachers in history, a man whose ideas still influence millions in every part of the world. However to grasp his importance not to religion but to information technology we need to understand not the whole of his religious message but the way in which he perceived himself. Although when we look at the earliest materials about him preserved in the ancient languages of South Asia and in Chinese we see that he felt he had a crucial message for the whole of humanity, he did not exactly view himself as the founder of a world religion. Rather, he felt that he had realised a truth that it was open to others to realise too, but that very few were capable both of realising for themselves and of communicating to their fellow human beings in such a way as to bring them also to the truth. Part of the reason for this was that arriving at the truth was not simply a matter of genius, as most people today would tend to construe it, but the outcome of prolonged religious dedication extending over many lifetimes attained through reincarnation. Correct moral behaviour, accumulating good karma, was the beginning of this process, since it was conducive to progress in meditation, which granted a heightened awareness, leading to wisdom.

This wisdom encouraged further devotion to morality, in a virtuous circle taking practitioners ever onwards and upwards, to the point in time when enlightenment freed them from delusion into a state unknown to our experience named nirvana.

The Buddha's early followers, and quite possibly the Buddha himself, believed that he had had no fewer than six predecessors as 'Enlightened Ones', and that following him an eighth Buddha, Maitreya, would appear in this world in due course.[1] But these figures are spread out across a vast history of the rise and fall of entire world systems, and even though Maitreya is destined to appear in this world, by most reckonings this will not be for tens of thousands of years. One day, perhaps, after many reincarnations, we may be fortunate enough to be born in human shape at a time when Maitreya is once more preaching the message of enlightenment, but we cannot count on it. Hence the heavy responsibility that weighed upon the Buddha during his religious career. For while he yet lived, he was able to help to bring many to enlightenment, speeding up their individual spiritual careers through the input of his teaching. But through his enlightenment he had broken the very bonds that kept him tied to the karmic wheel of reincarnation. So what would follow when his time on earth was ended and he entered the state of nirvana beyond this – or any other – world?

The obvious answer to us would be to write a book beforehand explaining our insights for the benefit of others. But at the time and in the place that the Buddha lived writing was not available. Culture, including the very early religious materials known as the Vedas, was carried from generation to generation by memory alone, so that a good education was essentially a form of mind training, not available to every man, let alone to women, but only to those high-status individuals with the leisure to devote to the task. The Buddha, or his followers, therefore had to devise their own system of making sure that his teachings were memorised, most especially since his ideas were very different from anything in the Vedas, and this implied the creation of a separate educational community devoted not simply to religious training in techniques of meditation and other practices but also to the maintenance of the Buddha's word. Recent scholarship has brought out the extent to which early Buddhist literature seems to have been deliberately formulated for oral preservation. Poetry is, of course, relatively easy to memorise, thanks to rhythm and rhyme, but to explicate the philosophical and often quite counter-intuitive concepts at the heart of Buddhism it was in general not the most suitable medium. Nor was it possible to eke out basic Buddhist teaching with improvisation, after the fashion of the tellers of epic tales throughout the world, who are usually given some liberty in filling out their performances. Repetition and other memory-enhancing devices there certainly are in early Buddhist literature, but the overall aim seems to have been to preserve the doctrines of the Buddha against the ravages of time.[2]

Given that one of the most basic initial insights of Buddhism is that all things must pass – more specifically, that all compound things are subject to change – the Buddhist community did not do a bad job. The Sangha or Buddhist clergy of monks and nuns effectively constituted a memory system, whose individual members might come and go, but who collectively could by dint of constant recitation over time keep the Buddha's word alive. Yet this sort of 'alive' was something of a second best, so it should occasion no surprise that another legacy of the Buddha also seems to have attracted the attention of his followers. For although the Buddha had died and been cremated, this was not the end of the story, in that his cremation resulted in relics; that is, in his continued physical existence in a different form. The notion of relics is also present in Christianity, especially medieval Christianity, and although the conceptions of what a relic is may differ between the two religions, they are close enough for the use of the English word in this context not to be entirely misleading. Again, recent scholarship has had much to say about the nature of relics in Buddhism, and views on the matter are far from unanimous.[3] But for immediate purposes it should be noted that the corporeal relics of the Buddha were conventionally said to number 84,000 fragments, which the great Buddhist ruler Ashoka had distributed across his empire so that this form of the Buddha's presence might benefit all his subjects. Yet the Buddha's relics were powerful enough in the view of many believers to be able to multiply in quantity even beyond this total, and for that matter to manifest themselves in the form of jewels rather than as fragments of bone.

The category of relic as used by Buddhists was broad, in that items such as the Buddha's bowl or robe with which he had become associated counted, as did for many the very shape of the Buddha, so that an image of the Buddha could count as a relic as well.[4] To judge from a passing reference by the early Christian writer, Clement of Alexandria, the cult of relics, which were customarily marked by the construction of stupas (Buddhist shrines) to house them, certainly struck outside observers of Indian Buddhism much more immediately than the recitation of texts. By the beginning of the Christian era, in fact, writing had become so widespread in China that Buddhist literature was now available in tangible form, and this may have encouraged those who felt that the teachings bequeathed by the Buddha were of more importance than any lingering form of corporeal presence to assert (or reassert) this view in a strong and concise fashion: 'He who has seen the Buddha's teachings has seen me.'[5] Such a linkage, however, could be construed in more than one way, especially in a situation in which the entire Buddhist tradition was evolving in new directions. By this time the unity of the tradition that had so successfully preserved the Buddha's teachings had become subject not only to scholastic disputes about how to understand those teachings but also to more fundamental disagreements as to aims and methods. These differences eventually gave rise to a distinct new form of Buddhism whose devotees gave it the general name of 'Mahayana', the 'Greater Vehicle' leading to salvation. The Mahayanist innovators dismissed those Buddhists who based themselves more narrowly on the literature transmitted since earlier times by the Sangha, as followers of a lesser means of achieving the same goal. The appearance of these innovators, and the nature of their initial preoccupations, is again the topic of intense study, though the eventual outcome of their efforts is clear enough, especially in the Buddhism of East Asia. The Buddha, for example, became far from the only figure to which one might look for spiritual succour, in that bodhisattvas, beings of immense spiritual power who postponed their own final enlightenment so that they might be more readily present to help the believer, were also held to be active in this world.

For our purposes, the most important aspect of the work of these innovators was their readiness to use writing to propagate their enlarged vision of what Buddhism was, and consequently their tendency to assign a very high value to the preservation and copying of written texts. 'He who has seen my teachings has seen me' in such circles could be construed to mean that the words of the Buddha, now rendered into a physical reality through writing, constituted relics of the Buddha's existence just as worthy of respect and veneration as any that had been transmitted in earlier times – if not more so. Their asseverations on this point gain added meaning in the light of recent scholarship which would suggest that, far from being an all-encompassing 'Greater Vehicle' sweeping away the conservative scholasticism of a few die-hards, the innovators themselves were a small minority of activists who desperately needed to get their message across to a wider audience. This preoccupation with copying texts becomes even more understandable when one considers the information technology they probably had at their disposal: fragile palm leaves that formed a natural, flat but highly vulnerable surface less robust even than papyrus, let alone paper.[6] Given the attrition rate for written materials of this sort, constant copying was much the best recommendation.

Although some scholars now feel that it may be wrong to see this urge to propagate the new ideas in writing as the most fundamental cause of their survival and ultimate success, it certainly must have helped their diffusion. By the end of the second century CE one finds the first text of this type translated into Chinese, complete with exhortations to view the result as equivalent to a shrine (that is, reliquary) of the Buddha and to copy it out and pass it on.[7] Soon enough writing is depicted – to Chinese Buddhists at least – as fundamental, for by the start of the fourth century it is possible to point to translations affirming that the canonical texts of the Buddhists had been written down from the time of their first organised compilation after the Buddha's death. The text specifies writing on silk scrolls, no less, even though silk was at this stage a strictly Chinese product; another translation of this period commends in the Chinese fashion copying the sacred text on bamboo and silk, again plainly a free rendering of the original Indian text.[8] Not long after, though, one finds surviving examples of Buddhist texts copied out on paper.

One of these, dated to CE 359, gives a good example of how Buddhist texts had already come to play a part in Chinese religious ritual, since a note at the end records exactly why, when and where it was written. Scholars have been able to confirm that it was the outcome of one of the innumerable bloody skirmishes that took place during this century of political fragmentation even when major warfare was not under way, for the good karma generated by copying the text is dedicated to the well-being of the spirits of those who had died in the conflict. Three religious factors have come together here: the Mahayana emphasis on the merit of copying; the Mahayana emphasis on the benefits of helping others to enlightenment, which allows that merit accrued by activities producing good karma can and indeed should be transferred; and an emphasis on the special need to see to the spiritual well-being of the deceased. The last-named factor would have been especially appreciated in

China, where ancestor-worship is attested to in the earliest written materials that have survived till the present day. To this way of thinking, those who died away from home or without descendants left spirits that would wander uncared for and cause problems for the living. Given the relentless violence of the period, creating an accumulation of merit that would take care of them through copying texts made excellent sense.[9]

But even though Buddhist scriptures fitted very well into the Chinese religious world because of their perceived value in such situations, the merit achieved by the act of copying by no means overshadowed the holy status of relic that the copy subsequently possessed. That the equivalence between Buddha's words and Buddha's holy relics was fully recognised in East Asia is clear from a whole range of materials, starting with miracle tales from China from about the fifth century onwards.[10] In the sixth century there is also a report that the containers for the earliest Buddhist texts supposed to have been brought to China under the Han dynasty were still receiving the worship due to relics, with 'incense regularly burned to them', in the temple in which they had been housed.[11] Manuscripts surviving from later times make a similar point in a more visual way, either by making the lines of text imitate the shape of a stupa, or by placing each character of the text in a stupa-shaped frame.[12] Since the Buddha's image was construed as a relic of the Buddha, in view of the close ties between relic and text it should come as no surprise that text and image were and are closely connected in Buddhist thought. The most graphic manifestations of this belief come from elsewhere in East Asia and somewhat later than the period of chief importance to the origins of printing, but again make the point plainly enough – most especially the example of a Japanese image inside which a sutra (Buddhist scripture) has been attached by springs right behind the eyes, animating the statue rather like a battery in a modern electrical device. Here the text is performing a function that in many images is performed by the inclusion of a corporeal relic of the Buddha, showing that in this role a text might end up somewhere where there was no possibility of anyone reading it at all.[13] It should be borne in mind that by 'anyone' most people today tend naturally to think only of 'anyone human', and that to contemporary ways of thinking spirits at the very least would have been able to read the text, as the Chinese – or so it seems from the early examples of 'unreadable' writing mentioned in the preceding chapter – had always believed from the start.

There is much about Buddhist ideas on sacred scripture as they were introduced to China that would have seemed perfectly intelligible to Chinese of the time if not to us, thanks to pre-existing tendencies within Chinese religion. Even the Taoist religion, which evolved to become Buddhism's main rival in China, shared many beliefs and practices with the foreign faith, occasionally as the result of imitation but usually because both groups of believers were part of a common culture that was developing under a wide range of influences at this time. As far as writing and manuscript culture were concerned, however, the Taoists looked back mainly to the imperial system created by the First Emperor and sustained by the Han dynasty as one of their models, since although Chinese dynasties ruled by virtue of the favour of the higher power of Heaven, their authority spanned what many today would see as distinct spiritual and temporal realms; an official, for example, had the power in theory to deal with minor malevolent spirits through exorcism. Although some religious groups had challenged Han political power in the second century CE, the Taoist tradition as it evolved came to confine itself to the spiritual sphere, carrying out exorcisms (to continue the example) in a private capacity as it were, but it still incorporated strong elements of bureaucracy in its attitudes and practices. A Taoist prayer, for example, was typically drawn up as a written bureaucratic petition to a superior; minor spirits were bossed about with bureaucratic orders in the name of higher authority. Taoist priests were experts in paperwork and procedure, and their method of transferring paperwork to the spirit world through burning (a practice based on sacrifice in other forms of Chinese religion) obviously distinguished their form of religious manuscript culture from the constant manuscript creation of the Buddhists.

But burning texts, or otherwise conveying texts to the spirit world through plunging them into deep water or hurling them skywards (a practice on which more will be said later) formed only a part of the Taoist involvement in the world of writing. It will be recalled from the preceding chapter that the spirits feared the use of writing by mankind because it might be used to put spells on them, and this was precisely what the Taoists did and do, using talismanic forms of Chinese characters possessed of more than ordinary efficacy.[14] These could be ritually created through freehand brush-strokes, but Taoists also found a role for seals in creating talismanic writing, occasionally using them to stamp messages dozens of characters long on surfaces such as soft clay. At the point where it is possible to be sure that the Taoists had transferred these stamping activities to paper, this plainly would have had some impact on the development of printing, and such evidence will also be discussed in due course. But one form of stamping used by the Taoists that the late Michel Strickmann investigated, and rather surprisingly found to have been known among Buddhists (apparently including Indian Buddhists) as well, does not involve the use of paper.[15] Instead, as part of a healing ritual, talismanic writing was stamped directly on the human body. This was no doubt preferable to the alternative of eating the writing on paper, since that method had caused severe constipation in at least one enthusiastic devotee until a Buddhist monk was called in to solve the problem.[16] In one sense the external application of stamped writing would have been even less conducive to the spread of printing as it is generally understood nowadays than the use of vellum, but one might argue that if the practice was widespread, it would have made the basic principles behind printing familiar to many. The use of seals in China was, however, not only ancient, but in the age of paper also very widespread: Chinese seals on paper simply use red ink, or even just black, and do not involve any special application of sealing wax or the like. As a result scores of examples more than a thousand years old – some as many as twenty characters long – may be found upon the surviving manuscripts from the Dunhuang archive.[17] By the period represented by the bulk of these manuscripts, seals had shifted from simple surfaces cut 'in intaglio', which left white images of the incised characters where the ink did not reach, to instruments in which the surface was cut away to leave characters standing in relief, so that the ink on them transferred their shapes alone to an otherwise unaffected piece of paper, much more in the manner of a wooden printing block. Art historians seem not to have investigated the nature of this shift closely, let alone pondered a possible link with the rise of printing, even though the key period seems to have been the seventh century. Nevertheless, it is interesting to note that one Buddhist in 730 distinguishes 'contemporary' seals cut in relief from older varieties.[18]

Taoists, however, did not have quite the same notion as the Buddhists concerning the role of sacred texts as equivalent to relics. They did not see their own sacred writings as something like 'Buddha's word', the legacy of a historical individual, but in order to compete with the foreign religion stressed much more that their scriptures were revelations from higher realms – in fact, their scriptures are represented as absolutely primordial, texts that existed in massive letters of fire before the beginning of the world.[19] But they are said to have worshipped their texts, at least before they took over the practice of image worship from the Buddhists.[20] There is also at least one case where an adept who appeared to die was discovered to have moved on to a higher spiritual plane when his coffin was opened and a written talisman was found inside. Even if more commonly swords or other objects were left behind, here at least a piece of writing does 'stand for' a holy person.[21] On the other hand, Buddhists did not exactly have talismanic writing that could overawe spirits by its very existence, even if some Buddhist scriptures of alleged Indian origin composed in East Asia do incorporate Chinese characters of a talismanic type.[22] They did, however, possess scriptures including, or even featuring as their main content, strings of syllables transcribed from Indian languages whose very sounds embodied immense power. Though the background to such texts in Buddhist thought is quite complex, the Chinese frequently referred to them straightforwardly as 'incantations' or even 'spells', and as this last translation of the Chinese term at least conveys how they were perceived by the general public, for the purposes of explaining the history of printing it is the term adopted here.

If, then, one looks back at the religious culture of China after the fall of the Han dynasty, it is possible to see much more that was conducive to the adoption of printing than can be found in the intellectual culture of the educated elite who served as bureaucrats under both the Chinese and non-Chinese regimes that sprang up to vie for the heritage of the Han empire. It would be wrong, of course, to suggest that these people with the skills to govern were in any way less interested in religion than the rest of their contemporaries. But they were simultaneously especially interested in cultivating their individuality in their cultural life, creating unique examples of inimitable calligraphy or densely allusive poems intelligible only to the well read. It was this commitment to high culture after all that defined their standing in society, even though actual power might at times be largely in the hands of military men, even warlords of foreign origin. Though the Chinese literati could and did copy books, multiple copying was a job for their clerical staff at the office. As devout believers they might also copy texts as a form of religious exercise, but their role as laypersons encouraged the sponsoring of sutra production carried out by others. In doing so they could of course be joined by anyone with the necessary means to participate, including the most brutal and illiterate warlords – perhaps especially the most brutal and illiterate warlords, if the clergy managed to persuade them that they had a particular need to atone for the bad karma created by their misdeeds.

The success of the Buddhist clergy in mobilising patronage was often spectacular. Vast sums of money must have been diverted to pay for the colossal images that still brood over the north Chinese landscape, carved from the living rock of its mountainsides, and one can only guess at the many gold and silver images that once existed before they were melted down in less pious times. But enough seems to have been left over to finance some extraordinary bibliographical enterprises: the creation, for instance, of multiple copies of the entire Buddhist canon, which even before it was augmented by further translations must have entailed the production of tens of thousands of scrolls. Of the half-dozen references to the copying of the entire canon in sets reaching double figures, the majority were ordered by emperors, and one may be permitted to doubt whether all that they ordered was ever achieved. Even so, a tiny fragment of a single surviving text from a set of sixteen canons ordered by a mere imperial relative still exists, and specifically states that ten copies had already been made.[23] Such was the result of Mahayana exhortations to earn merit through copying when transferred from stylus and palm leaf to brush and paper. Yet if one turns to the European situation, even on the eve of the introduction of printing, Elizabeth Eisenstein appears to doubt that far less spectacular orders for multiple copies of manuscript texts were ever met in full, even though she is talking of a mere two to four hundred copies of rather short books.[24] It cannot be doubted that productivity in China was far higher: early manuscripts of the *Lotus Sutra* – at seven scrolls, not a particularly short book, and one that fills a decent sized volume in English translation – may be found in China bearing the meticulous notation 'one thousand, seven hundred and eighty-fourth copy' and 'one thousand eight hundred and seventh copy'.[25] References to thousands of copies will be encountered again below; there is no need to think that they are exaggerated, nor that they imply the use of printing.

But if, by the end of the fifth century, the Buddhists had both the manpower and the motives to create multiple copies, the Taoists had the method. Buddhists were familiar with seals, which were known from early times in India too, but Taoists, whose beliefs were heavily tinged with notions of authority, made much more use of them in religious contexts – not simply in healing, but for example in their practice of alchemy.[26] Taoists would make multiple copies of seals known to have carried quite lengthy texts: on one occasion several hundred copies of one such seal, impressed on clay, are said to have been lobbed into a deep pool to polish off a water monster.[27] But this 'printing' only multiplied the text for application to one specific problem, just as with the use of seals in healing. There seems to be no thought of distributing the created text for future use. In some ways the Taoist uses of text bring out yet more clearly than the Buddhist ones the extremely broad range of uses of texts that could be important within the religious world of China after the Han era. Texts were not simply reading materials, but could, like the indulgences printed by Gutenberg, perform more practical and immediate religious functions. This might involve them in being burned, drowned, eaten or hidden in inaccessible places, since their messages were not necessarily directed at human beings. Buddhist texts worked as holy objects, too, but were always to a minimal extent reading materials at the same time; even the texts based on spells normally included some narrative concerning the efficacy of the unintelligible syllables that constituted the spell itself.

Just one more factor was required in the dynamic, unstable, multi-ethnic and multicultural world of post-Han China to pull all these elements together and result in the establishment of wood-block printing as an independent technology. That factor was fear, and not merely the individual, everyday levels of fear concerning death, judgment and the torments of Hell that affected anyone familiar with the detailed and intimidating pictures of the afterlife now propounded by Buddhist and Taoist doctrine. In the middle of the sixth century, precisely when some stability seemed to be returning for the first time in centuries, a new shadow fell across China – and across Europe too, from the Celtic lands of Britain to the Bosporus. Historians today are just beginning to appreciate the enormity of this event, and of the despondency it caused. Its effects can be detected in Bede's writings, though to get closer to the mid-sixth century it is necessary to turn to another figure whom he mentions as a sort of predecessor, a British monk named Gildas.

CHAPTER FOUR

THE RUIN OF BRITAIN

If anyone remembers the verbose and dyspeptic writings of Gildas today, it is not for their literary merit, nor yet for his rather limited value as a narrative historian, but because of his apparent indirect testimony to the existence of someone infinitely more famous, the heroic King Arthur.[1] Curiously, he does not mention him by name; rather, as a prologue to his animadversions on the inadequacy of British leadership in his own times, bluntly entitled *The Ruin of Britain,* he simply recapitulates the story of the collapse of Roman rule and the terrible times that ensued in the fifth century before indicating that a great victory against their Anglo-Saxon foes in the early sixth century had eventually provided a period of respite, which in the mid-century he now saw threatened by internecine strife. It is only in later sources that the victor who had provided this respite is named as Arthur. But however imprecise Gildas may be, when his writings are compared with those of contemporaries further east – in Byzantium, and in north and south China – an interesting pattern emerges that modern advances in our ability to reconstruct the past climate of our planet have begun to make sense of, in a way that was evidently hidden from Gildas himself.

For lamentations about the sudden withering away of promising signs of long-sought-for stability may be found in the writings of several of his contemporaries across the globe. The great Byzantine historian Procopius, for example, whose official writings celebrate the many splendid achievements of the Emperor Justinian, also penned – for the benefit of posterity alone – a work known as *The Secret History,* giving his private, vitriolic and highly personal addendum to that story, and indicating how very deeply disappointed he became with Justinian's rule. In China any expression of disillusion with imperial rule is always much harder to find. But following its abandonment due to internal conflict in 534, one does find overwhelming sentiments of regret over the lost glories of the northern capital of Luoyang lovingly detailed by a writer named Yang Xuanzhi. The rifts within the northern Chinese polity, which were clearly serious enough to tear the country apart whatever the weather was up to, eventually spilled over into the south, after one losing general sought refuge there. Under normal circumstances one defector, however ambitious, might not have caused too much trouble. But by the middle of the century the originally much more secure southern regime was also tumbling towards collapse, with warfare spread far and wide, dislocating society from top to bottom and resulting in one of the most famous poems of regret in Chinese, the 'Lament for the South' composed in northern captivity by the former southern gentlemen Yu Xin.

In itself the appearance of four pieces of writing in a distinctly negative vein, written across the world within the space of a few decades, could easily count as coincidence, even from a century that has bequeathed much less to modern readers than more recent times. But the modern study of historical climate change, drawing on such evidence as tree rings and ice core samples, has put Gildas and his contemporaries in a new context. The pattern of decline and fall in East and West that seems to mark the second to fifth centuries of the first millennium CE becomes much more intelligible when set against climate evidence such as (for China) the freezing of the Gulf of Bohai, an arm of the Yellow Sea. By the start of the sixth century, however, the climate seems to have improved, and for the first time in as long as anyone could remember life for a while became almost pleasant – on the streets of Luoyang it was possible to buy oranges traded up from the south, a sure indication of relative peace. But in 536, suddenly and against the prevailing climate trend, everything went very wrong. In Europe Procopius and other chroniclers noted that the light of the sun was obscured for over a year, evidently by some sort of 'dry fog' of dust particles. Soon thereafter plague arrived, eventually (apparently a bit later than the time Gildas was writing) spreading all the way across the continent to Britain. In China the political instability that had already caused the evacuation of Luoyang was rapidly accelerated by famine: the sources tell of destitute mobs, like 'flocks of crows', rallying in rebellion against the still affluent rulers of the south, eventually capturing the emperor himself and starving him to death.

The most probable cause for all this – a massive volcanic eruption (possibly at Rabaul, on New Britain, off the east coast of New Guinea) producing a sort of 'nuclear winter' – was identified more than two decades ago, but it is only much more recently that data relating this to East Asia have been reported in the scientific literature.[2] Factoring the consequences of this event into our existing narratives of East Asian history is a task that has not really begun, and much work needs to be done before it will be possible to arrive at a reasonable appreciation of its impact. Within the unfolding narrative of East Asian religious history, however, enough information exists to hazard the suggestion that the psychological consequences in terms of feelings of insecurity (indeed, not only mere feelings of insecurity, given the bloody chaos of the age) were nothing short of profound. Admittedly, producing evidence that might allow us to quantify these feelings is a little tricky. Things had been so bad for so long before the start of the sixth century that everyone in China was more than familiar with the notion that the end of the world was at hand, so no completely new sensations of doom are detectable in our sources, which tend to use the language already established concerning disaster and the uncertainties of the future. Buddhist and Taoist beliefs were somewhat different, though the popular mind more often than not absorbed elements of both ways of thinking. In Taoism the end of the current dispensation in history was expected in the near future, with fire, flood and warfare typically sweeping away the corrupt rulers of the age and forging the path for a utopian world populated by the devout, who would survive this time of tribulation. Buddhists in China received from India the idea that all things must pass, but on a far longer time scale. This outlook was much bleaker: the influence of the historical Buddha, Shakyamuni, was destined to fade slowly, to the point where all the relics and all the texts he had bequeathed would disappear, emptying the world of all spiritual meaning. The only hope for Buddhists was – and (with some qualifications) still is – to keep on undergoing reincarnation in this progressively less supportive environment until after thousands of years the next Buddha, Maitreya, appears and renews the possibility of enlightenment. No wonder that many Buddhists in China who had not been indoctrinated by the clergy in the 'correct' understanding of the future received from India preferred to adopt the more dramatic but ultimately also more reassuring view of their Taoist rivals.

One consequence was that by the sixth century Chinese regimes in north and south were well acquainted with the disruption that could be caused by desperate peasants roused to action by a variety of figures who might be characterised as 'false messiahs'. Recently it has been pointed out that one of these may have been of some importance to the history (or prehistory) of printing.[3] In the histories of south China the record tells of a certain Gong Xuanxuan, who 'said that a supernatural being had given him a "jade seal jade block writing", which did not require a brush: one blew on the paper and characters formed. He called himself Gong the Sage, and used them to mislead the masses', even deluding one local governor, though his successor dealt with him according to the law – which would imply execution. The date indicated seems to be some time in the 480s. Now I would agree with the discoverers of this very interesting record that it suggests a move away from the limitations of using a hand-held seal to stamp text or image on to paper below towards the use of a larger block, to which paper is applied from above. But I doubt that the invention of the printing block in itself would have allowed Gong to claim to be a sage and dupe even an educated official. Evidence for the taking of impressions from incised inscriptions – which was a very popular practice in later China for disseminating the precise calligraphy of famous inscriptions, including those of the First Emperor – cannot be found until the early sixth century, but the assumption is that the practice goes back somewhat earlier.[4] The technique for taking rubbings is admittedly different from that employed by woodblock printers, since the underlying text is not cut in reverse. But even so I cannot believe that the use of a block was so radical an advance that the masses were amazed. What does seem to have been amazing was the appearance of characters on paper as the result of blowing on it: a very light pressure which suggests that Gong's expertise was much more in the use of 'secret inks' that would reveal themselves in response to such a stimulus. By the time the report was written up, moreover, taking an imprint from reversed characters on an inscription was also known, but the odd and clumsy term 'jade seal jade block writing' further suggests that the historian had not heard of anything else quite like this device.[5] Gong seems to have used the process to deliberately mystify onlookers, whereas the product itself does not seem to have been so important. That is presumably why a high-quality material like jade was used, though perhaps the trick with the ink (if that is what it was) would not have worked with wood. Even so, if Gong could do what he is said to have done, he could have been China's first printer. It just seems that he wanted to be a bit more mysterious than that, and that he paid the price for his presumption.

So to understand the background to the rise of printing it is necessary to return once more to religious history, and specifically to the volatile religious environment of the late sixth century. Although it has been stressed that the Chinese religious tradition was continuous, and that many of the ideas and practices character-istic of the late sixth century were inherited from earlier times, it is still possible to point to one or two novelties, and significantly enough one of them concerned religious texts. Because Buddhists were oppressed by the fear that the Buddha's words would pass away from this world, Buddhist scripture began to be carved on mountain stone with the specific aim of making it permanent in a way that writing on paper was not. By the seventh century this activity had become particularly associated with one centre not far from present day Beijing, the Yunju si, where over subsequent centuries much of the vast bulk of the Buddhist canon came to be carved on stone slabs.[6] One might almost call this the opposite of printing, so labo-rious does the project seem. But it does testify eloquently to the fears of the age and suggest the very high anxiety that was there to be exploited by false messiahs, just as much as other novelties such as cults involving self-flagellation for one's sins and similar indications of religious extremism.

Now this highly volatile religious atmosphere clearly posed a problem for the rulers of the age, for whom the shaking up of the status quo of the early part of the century actually provided fresh opportunities for conquest, if they could only exploit them – in fact north China was reunited in 577, and the north conquered the south in 589. But although small-time messiahs like Gong Xuanxuan could be eliminated by violence, in order to bend their populations to their will and to curb their fears successive regimes at this time also pursued clear religious policies designed to portray themselves in a messianic light. This was in a sense nothing new: in fifth-century north China, the notion that emperor and Buddha were ultimately one and the same was given iconographic form in the colossal stone figures that still survive at the Yungang Caves.[7] More subtly, the ruler of south China during the early sixth century – the very monarch who was later starved to death – tried to place himself at the head of the Buddhist clergy.[8] In both cases one may detect behind the imagery used the figure of Ashoka, regarded as a Chakravartin or 'Wheel-turning King', endowed with the same ancient South Asian symbol of imperial power that may be found on the national flag of India even today.[9] The Buddhist conception of the Chakravartin had for a good while a profound influence on Chinese political ideas, although Chinese political philosophy before modern times has generally been discussed without any reference whatsoever to earlier outside influences.[10] But by the start of the seventh century the prevailing religious climate made it necessary not simply to allay fears about the passing away of the Buddha's word but also to bring the popular understanding of the emperor's role as close to that of Ashoka as possible.[11]

The former aim, that of allaying fear of the loss of Buddha's word, was quite easily met by the prevailing manuscript technology of information that has already been described: during the lifetime of the emperor who reigned from 604 to 618 no fewer than 900,000 scrolls had been copied under imperial auspices; his father, Emperor Wendi of the Sui dynasty, the reunifier of China, had himself already sponsored the copying of 130,000 scrolls, a feat that his bureaucracy probably took quite easily in its stride, since at the time of the conquest of the south they had provided him already with 300,000 copies of the imperial edict denouncing his opponent. It is unfortunate that the nomads who brought rumours of the reunification of China to Byzantium were in all probability illiterate, for if they had been able to convey any inkling of such vast literary productivity to the West it would no doubt have made even more of an impact than their tales of great cities and tree-lined waterways far away. Wendi had also taken steps to demonstrate his power by emulating the great Ashoka on a somewhat lesser scale through the distribution of Buddha relics, again something that the Byzantines' informants would not have noticed, though they did comment on the many images to be found in China.

Given, however, that Ashoka was supposed to have distributed 84,000 Buddha relics, the Chinese effort at this time appears to have concentrated much more on quality rather than quantity, since our sources on the episode mention just 107 relics, dispatched only to the major local administrative units out of the 190 units that formed the reunited empire, though there are some indications that some of China's neighbours were favoured with the gift of relics too.[12] The choice of 107 relic installations was probably quite deliberate, since with one central, metropolitan relic added they would have made up a total pattern of 108 significant stupas, a Buddhist number symbolically addressing all the possible woes of mankind. Later examples of this symbolic number certainly have been identified.[13] The enshrinement of these relics, in three separate batches, to the accompaniment of seven days of ceremonies conducted by as many as 360 monks at any one place must have created a lavish spectacle announcing to the new empire the vast powers of religious patronage at its ruler's disposal. Even better, imperial propagandists lost no time in recording various miracles associated with the enshrinement of the relics at their destinations, thus enhancing the religious prestige of the dynasty throughout the land. Though the would-be Chakravartin's son, for all his sponsoring of Buddhist copyists, rapidly squandered all the merit accrued by launching upon foreign wars and on civic works such as canal building so colossal in scale as to provoke the population to rebellion and seal his own fate. Since this process of complete unravelling only took a decade and a half, memories of the imperially sponsored distribution of relics no doubt remained strong amongst the subjects of the new rulers who, in 618, eventually inherited the vast empire thrown up by the turmoil of the late sixth century.[14]

These rulers, who preserved due caution with regard to keeping the population on their side, provided the stability that allowed the reunited empire not simply to benefit from what seem to have become – for all the sudden shock of the 536 incident – somewhat better climate conditions but also, once the effects of civil war had been overcome, to prosper. Even so, prosperity by no means reached levels leading to universal contentment, and it may be that the strains of uneven economic development actually exacerbated the pessimistic mood that had emerged earlier in religious circles. At any rate, the notion that the influence of Buddhism was destined to fade away was in itself so impeccably orthodox that one may consider strategies to combat this negative prospect one of the key elements in the unfolding of Buddhist ideas at this time. Thus one finds state-sponsored exegetical schools very much in favour of the idea that space and time are not what they seem, but rather consti-tute a vast interconnected unity, with the corollary that links to the time and place of the Buddha's enlightenment may be found in the here and now by anyone with the right religious training. Those of a less philosophical disposition, of course, remained vulnerable to the blandishments of a new generation of false messiahs, making the need for the new dynasty to assert its religious credentials as urgent as it had ever been.

Perhaps all the pomp and circumstance of the relic distributions of the beginning of the seventh century seemed at first – in the light of the rapid collapse of the preceding dynasty – too hubristic to be revived at once. Certainly religious policy from 618 onwards gives the impression of having initially made very cautious progress. In general outlook the new ruling house, which bore the surname Li, was quite close to its predecessors and even to the rulers that had been supplanted in the north by Wendi of the Sui dynasty, he who reunified China. All of them were military men from a culture heavily influenced by intermarriage with the Inner Asian warrior peoples who had entered China from the fourth century onwards: reasonably devout, but also practical. Religion was something to be used, but in view of the continuing volatility of the religious situation, the Li family seems to have felt that it should be used cautiously. The fact that they shared their family name with Laozi, the great sage of Taoism, considered by all devout Taoists an avatar of the highest divinity, did encourage them to trace their descent from him, thus affirming both their Chinese identity and also a form of legitimacy by divine descent, somewhat like that until recently affirmed by the imperial family of Japan.[15] In the first half of the seventh century, every indication is that this idea was not formulated in such a way as to threaten their simultaneous patronage of Buddhism. This patronage was not, however, as lavish as before, and it is not possible to find in this period any obvious signs that the emperors of the new line wished to emulate Ashoka.

Nevertheless, by this time ways of creating relics – or their equivalents as objects of worship and spiritual reassurance – that did not depend on a lavish panoply of ceremonial and material display had been in existence for some time, and had developed elsewhere to a point where the creation of 84,000 relics of a more modest sort, or even of many more, was a realistic possibility. After all, a relic did not have to be encased in a golden casket and installed in a stupa the size of a house, nor did the relic itself have to be a substantial fragment of Buddha's bone: there were such relics, but they acted as the focus of worship pulling in pilgrims over a wide area. More common or garden (literally) structures also existed – one early Chinese pilgrim going to India noted that in Khotan there were stupas outside every house, though he does not say what was in them.[16] It was not even necessary for them to be structured as containers, nor to have anything inside them: in the early fifth century in the north-west of the Chinese cultural area there was one type of stupa consisting only of a short pillar shape, ranging from less than a foot to over three feet in height. There is nothing inside; rather, it must be the images on the outside, such as those carved around the octagonal lowest layer of the structure, that function as relics. Even more likely, the relics of the Buddha are constituted by the text – inscribed typically on the next layer above this octagonal base – that summarizes the most basic core of the Buddha's teachings.[17] But this is by no means the only type of 'reliquary' (if that is how one is to understand 'stupa') with nothing inside: later types of stone pillar elsewhere in China function in the same way, and there are signs that all freestanding stones – steles, to use the art historians' term – with Buddha images or text on them were ritually regarded as equivalent to stupas.[18]

Here, then, it is possible to find solid testimony that Buddhists of this era took seriously the idea that image or text could function as a form of the Buddha's presence. But in that case, how small could a stupa or locus of Buddha presence be? The question is more than merely speculative: the Mahayana emphasis on the simultaneous existence of a multitude of Buddhas was by the early sixth century well represented in Chinese Buddhist art, with so-called 'thousand Buddha' patterns of multiple small images imported from further west – usually, however, in conjunction with larger single figures.[19] The early examples extant today are all carved out of stone, but obviously in order to create a multiplicity of small images – or passages of text – mechanical means such as moulds, stencils or stamps would have commended themselves as aids to greater productivity. The use of moulds to make Buddhist images in China was well established by the sixth century, and Buddhist texts translated from Sanskrit incorporate metaphors based on pattern transfer by moulds, evidently envisaging a lost wax method of casting, suggesting that the technology was widely understood.[20] Moulds for making parts of images of clay survive from Central Asia, and 'pounces', a form of stencil using powder and perforated paper to create preparatory outlines for multiple Buddha images, survive among the Dunhuang manuscripts recovered in the early twentieth century after more than a thousand years, along with examples of the final results in adjoining cave temples, though it is unclear when this type of device first came into use.[21] A stamped image of the Buddha dating apparently to about 500 with Sanskrit text attached has been found on one Chinese manuscript, though there is no way to show that this isolated instance forms part of the systematic multiple creation of Buddha relics.[22] But the clearest evidence for the multiple manufacture of stupas by mechanical means does not come from China, but from India from the late sixth century onwards, and concerns miniatures made out of clay, with a textual epitome of Buddhism stamped on to them; the epitome is, in fact, a short formula that had already been in use for several centuries as a form of textual relic substitute.[23] Two (probably) slighter later developments also need to be remarked on at this point. First, it is also possible to find, in place of the text epitomising the Buddha's insight on them, texts of a rather later type embodying extraordinary spiritual power: as explained above, the Chinese, somewhat simplifying the significance of these, tended to translate the term used to denote this type of text with a word meaning 'a spell', for they were based on mystic syllables that were simply transliterated into Chinese to preserve their power, but were as meaningful to a Chinese reader as 'abracadabra' is to a reader of English today. Amongst the benefits promised by these texts, however, was that the creation of a single stupa incorporating a copy of this sort of written material was, in terms of good karma, worth ten million of the ordinary sort.[24] Secondly, the creation of miniature stupas and like objects (of which the Tibetan *tsha-tsha* is the best known) related frequently to funerary practices, often through the incorporation of the ashes of cremated persons into their manufacture.[25]

We can only guess at the circumstances that prompted the initial introduction of these mass-manufactured items, for to assume that the climate change shock that affected Europe and East Asia and prompted religious changes in both had a similar impact in South Asia is as yet somewhat unsafe.[26] Chinese archaeological researchers do, however, appear to confirm that although miniature Buddha figures from before the seventh century may be found on Chinese soil, there is no evidence that miniature stupas were created in China at such an early date.[27] In any case, to the extent that the multiple creation and perhaps (though this cannot be proved) distribution of the same text by mechanical means constitute printing, then this Indian practice must be seen as an important part of the prehistory of the technology. That the text was not created as a piece of reading matter but so as to constitute a relic seems to me not to form a serious objection to this assertion, for the stamped verses remained in principle readable as much by a human as by a supernatural being. Only the materials used – like the ceramic materials used by the First Emperor – appear as something of a dead end, for while small clay objects can be distributed readily enough, sufficient stamped clay to form a book would be a vulnerable medium for the large-scale dissemination of knowledge, even if clay tablets were used in the ancient Near East to archive knowledge.

We should not forget, however, that Buddhism, for all the innovations it inspired, was not the only organised religious tradition to affect the development of Chinese material culture. The technological elements in image and text creation considered above were also well known to the Taoists of this era, and some time around the middle of the seventh century it is possible to find in a text evidently designed to promote higher standards amongst monastic Taoists – still probably very much a minority amongst Taoists of the day, since monasticism was basically a borrowing from their Buddhist rivals – a list of acceptable materials out of which to create a religious image.[28] One or two of these must have caused the Buddhists a moment or more of reflection: the manufacture of holy snowmen, for example, since although snowmen are mentioned in passing in translated Buddhist texts available by the seventh century, there is no suggestion that such impermanent icons might be suitable for worship. Nor is there any suggestion that good Buddhists might create a Buddha image by stamping it on paper as, according to this source, the Taoists explicitly saw fit to do. It has already been noted that a stamped Buddha image survives from a century and a half earlier than this, but since this was superimposed on a holy text, perhaps it only counted as added decoration in terms of the explicit norms observed by the Chinese clergy, however the pious laity might have viewed it. Their Indian texts, of course, made no mention of paper where the predominant writing culture still relied on palm leaves.

So by the time that the house of Li had consolidated its grip on China, religious and technological developments in the wake of the great climate shock of 536 had evolved in various directions that might be construed as favourable to the emergence of printing. What happened next, however, resulted not so much from further advances in religion or technology in general as from the dynastic politics of the Li family itself, and it is to these that we must now turn.

CHAPTER FIVE

THE LIVES AND LOVES OF THE LI FAMILY

As the middle of the seventh century approached, the old emperor was tired and anxious, not least about the matter of succession. No dynasty within living memory had survived longer than its fourth decade, which the Tang dynasty founded by the Li family had now entered. The youth barely out of his teens whom he had selected as his heir was not a man after his own heart – warfare, hunting and drinking were of less interest to him than to other sons whom the anxious father had been forced to pass over. Yet to his published political testament to the young man the father added a personal postscript frankly admitting that his own conduct should not be taken as a model.[1] This was undoubtedly sound advice: he had reached the throne by personally killing one of his brothers in a coup that hustled his own father, the capable founder of the dynasty, into early retirement. A usurpation of this kind was not unknown during this turbulent era of Chinese history, but direct fratricide (as opposed to bringing false charges against a rival in the hope of his execution) was harder to explain away, and the old emperor had been much exercised as to how to influence historians so as to gloss over the matter. As things turned out, he need not have worried: his later descendants needed a golden age to look back to, and they presented the emperor's public efforts at displaying a consensual approach to government, always ready to take advice from his ministers, as the very picture of how China ought to be run.

Fortunately for the old man, he had combined this temporary effort at reining in his autocratic disposition with generally successful military leadership, for the first time since the glory days of the Han, expanding Chinese influence far to the west along the trade routes skirting the deserts of Central Asia. Today many people – and not just Westerners – have become accustomed to thinking of these routes as constituting a Silk Road to Europe. But it is worth remembering that that designation is a nineteenth-century European invention: for most Chinese, the trade routes, turning south at the far side of the desert, brought them into contact with a then more important mythic West that was the heartland of Buddhism. Early in the emperor's reign, for example, one Chinese monk had defied border regulations to slip away on a journey that took him right to the places where the Buddha had preached, and to the great university of Buddhist learning nearby in which he studied for a decade and a half. When he returned in 645 he was proficient in Sanskrit and in Buddhist Studies (including topics such as logic, scarcely known in China) and carried with him a multitude of Buddhist (and even one or two non-Buddhist) texts: by the time he died in 664 his translations filled over 1,300 scrolls, yet it is recorded that he left plenty of material he never got round to translating. Even what he did achieve on his return would have been impossible without the emperor's support, though while his epic travels have inspired and continue to inspire many Chinese, it seems the emperor was chiefly impressed by the intelligence he was able to provide about the lands beyond the borders of the Tang empire.[2] Though the emperor may have changed his outlook as his eventual death in 649 approached, for most of his reign he withheld conspicuous patronage from the Buddhists, and the only scripture he had

had copied out and distributed throughout his empire was a short text supposedly giving the Buddha's final instructions to his disciples that has been suspected of being a Chinese product telling monks how they ought to behave.[3]

Even so, the monk had brought back from India a wealth of knowledge that included first-hand reports of how massive numbers of miniature stupas were being manufactured there: he describes how one great Indian teacher sponsored the creation of 700,000 tiny stupas, each housing a short passage of text, grouped one hundred thousand at a time in seven much larger stupas.[4] But the monk was not the only visitor to India at this time: one government official is recorded as having gone via the much shorter but more difficult route through Tibet on repeated diplomatic missions to the kingdoms of India at the behest of both the old emperor and later of his heir.[5] He, too, brought back both information and more tangible souvenirs of his trip, including eventually in 660 a relic consisting of a portion of the skull bone of the Buddha, plus other objects including four 'Buddha seals', meaning no doubt stamps for creating Buddha figures out of clay.[6] There is firm evidence that these contacts (or the more anonymous contacts achieved by traders working these routes) swiftly resulted in the large-scale multiple production of small Buddha images in China, for a number of examples have been found in the region of the then Chinese capital of a clay representation of the Buddha bearing on the reverse a message stating that the monk Falü (otherwise unknown) made 84,000 of them for the benefit of the dynasty and of his ancestors, in the year 650.[7] So the mass creation of objects on an Ashokan scale was not a problem – indeed, even under the brief preceding dynasty one leading monk was said to have sponsored the creation of 100,000 gilded and painted wooden images – but a private citizen would have hesitated no doubt to take the step of deliberately distributing them across the country, for that would have had clear imperial overtones.[8]

By 650, however, a new emperor had just ascended the throne, and he would have been far more interested in such matters than his father. It has sometimes been surmised that the reason that the old emperor's advisers insisted on the young man becoming heir apparent was because they thought him more pliable – his mother was in fact the daughter of one of them. But one doubts that the old emperor would have given in to their demands if he thought that was their objective. Rather, it seems that even his father had reluctantly come to the conclusion that now that the dynasty had established itself by force of arms, a period of consolidation was necessary in which attention might be paid to articulating a ruling ideology: that is, to proclaiming to the population arguments demonstrating Heaven's divine favour towards the dynasty and making clear that it was both right and proper to acquiesce in rule by the Li family. For this task intellectual subtlety was obviously going to be of greater importance than martial prowess, and it was perhaps this quality that his father and the new emperor's father's advisers had seen in him. At the same time he seems to have been remarkably short on megalomania; others in East Asia who posed as Chakravartin kings or divine descendants of Taoist gods could (and did) succumb to the power of these beliefs to the extent of ending up being destroyed by them. The old man, however, seems to have brought up his son in the family tradition of using religion, not of being used by it. Still, the prospect of deliberately taking steps, however prudently, to raise oneself to a higher spiritual plane than the rest of one's subjects would have seemed a tricky and a lonely path to follow, and one would not be surprised to find the young emperor looking for a confidante, someone who could understand what he was doing and yet not use that knowledge against him.

He certainly found a friend. He found the woman I have described in Bede's imaginary vision in the first chapter of this book. There she was introduced as a former concubine of his father, the daughter of an early supporter of the dynasty, who had come to his attention while his father still lived.[9] Although histories started to be carefully compiled from daily court diaries during the young emperor's reign, it should be borne in mind that at the best of times what went on inside the imperial palace would never have been transparent to the bureaucrats who lived outside it, and that for much of the more lurid details of her life all the authors of our sources would have had to rely on second-hand evidence. But it seems indubitable that she had served as one of the palace ladies of his father, though her role may have amounted to no more than that of a lady in waiting, even if all such women were potential concubines of the emperor. Fortunately, seventh-century China took a more relaxed view of who was suitable as an imperial consort than would have been the case in later times: once the young emperor had brought her back to the palace there were complaints, but everyone knew that there were also precedents for bending the rules. While his father was still alive, however, they both ran something of a risk, given the readiness of rivals both amongst the imperial princes and the palace ladies to denounce even imaginary derelictions to the emperor in the hope of self-advancement. This suggests that the young woman possessed not only a captivating beauty but also a considerable determination.

Sources on her father make it clear that she came from exactly the same north-western group of families as both the Li family and its immediate predecessors – her mother was even related to the family of the man who had reunified China. But it was later rumoured that her father had in his early days dabbled in the timber business, something a true aristocrat would have shunned. The family name was Wu; not, however, the most common name so transcribed, but a more unusual one meaning 'martial'. This word was also an honorary epithet often applied to kings and emperors, and thus a bit like the name 'Strong' in English, which similarly serves as a family name and as the translation of a royal epithet from European history. Since she did eventually take the title of emperor it might seem that 'Emperor Wu' should be the correct way to refer to her, rather than the 'Empress Wu', which is the title used in most English-language writing about her. 'Emperor Wu', however, invites confusion with various other rulers who attracted the honorary epithet – the unfortunate imitator of Ashoka who was starved to death, for example – and so most Western historians have baulked at giving her the ruling title she actually awarded herself, though in East Asian languages it is possible to distinguish 'empress as female emperor' from 'empress as imperial consort'. But her family name seems to have been found so apt by contemporaries and by their descendants that it stuck fast, outlasting even the semi-divine titles that she invented for herself: a ninth-century Japanese visitor found her referred to simply as 'Granny Strong'.

Concerning her youth, as the unknown 'Lady Strong', it is extremely hard to find any concrete details, but one intriguing fact has emerged from recent research. Most Chinese historians appear to have believed that she was born in 624, but some years ago I pointed to aspects of her religious behaviour compatible with astrological beliefs suggesting that she was born in 628, a possibility countenanced by some revisionist scholarship.[10] A recent Chinese study, based on entirely different evidence, has come to the same conclusion.[11] What this means is that although she was exactly the same age as the young emperor, her contemporaries formed the impression right from the start, when they were both barely twenty, that she was several years older than him. Again this suggests a young person who was remarkably self-possessed.

She needed to be. The year before the old emperor's death, a prophecy swept the palace that a woman named the Martial (i.e. Wu) King would one day deprive the Li family of its imperial heritage. Fortunately for her, that any woman could achieve kingship was, it seems, literally quite unthinkable amongst the political elite in China at that time, even though the culture allowed women more autonomy than under some later dynasties. But the old emperor did not like to take risks with the future of his family, and when it was discovered that a general had been nicknamed 'Fifth Lady' in his youth, this was enough to get him executed. It is worth noting, however, that this did not put a stop to the prophecy, and that amongst the general population the notion of a female ruler was clearly not as unthinkable as among the elite, for four years later, in 653, there is a record of a woman warrior (apparently unaware of the prophecy, since she did not use the term Wu in her title) rising in rebellion as emperor, and even gathering enough of a following to cause widespread disruption in the weeks before her inevitable defeat and death.[12]

By this time young Lady Strong was making good progress towards her immediate goal of becoming the main consort of her husband. She was lucky enough to give birth to at least one son by the following year, and this strengthened her hand considerably against the unfortunate childless lady who had been formally designated as empress, and against another rival. It was at this point, the sources tell us, that ministers connected with these other women argued forcefully against 'Lady Strong', in part because of her former employment by the old emperor. But by the end of 655 false accusations against her rivals for the emperor's affections had achieved her goal, and both were dead, allegedly killed with great cruelty at her instigation, while their relatives and supporters in the bureaucracy were swiftly purged. That the emperor was prepared to tolerate this change to the appearance of consensual government that had characterised his father's reign suggests that he already saw in her a measure of political wisdom that made broader consultation unnecessary, though later historians would have us believe that he was simply retreating into the role of hen-pecked husband that they see as his destined fate from the start.

Whatever his thoughts about Lady Strong's ruthlessness, the record suggests that the conventional scholarly historians responsible for this image, imbued to a man with bitter hatred for the woman who dared eventually to usurp the male prerogative of imperial rule, could not see the emperor's achievements objectively. His armies, for example, did well in consolidating his father's conquests, so although he did not personally engage in bloodshed in the manner of his forebears, he did prove a successful military leader. And as early as 656 he began taking steps to consolidate the ideological position of the dynasty as well, by starting to merge the terminology of traditional imperial sacrificial observances with that of the Taoist religion.[13] The coincidence of the Li family name with one much honoured within that religion (which had already produced a good number of false messiahs using the name) after all encouraged the progressive use of Taoist symbolism to create a family cult elevating the status of the Lis to that of rulers by hereditary divine right.

But although the emperors of the Tang dynasty were always prepared to give precedence to Taoists on the impeccable grounds of filial piety towards their divine ancestor, at this stage the new emperor was still pragmatic enough to make use of Buddhist symbolism as well. The figure of Ashoka seems to have fascinated both him and his newly installed empress – perhaps in her case a paragon of Buddhist rule was much more interesting than the idea of a divine line of descent that did not include her. One source, written later in her life, even attributes an interest in Ashoka to her father, who does indeed seem to have been an occasional patron of Buddhism. The well-established penchant for discovering Buddhist relics on Chinese soil supposedly dating back to the time when Ashoka ruled the entire world had in any case resulted in the emergence of a number of cult centres associated with his name, including one in the north-west already known to the powerful families of the area from whom the imperial couple were descended. It is furthermore quite clear that when the attention of the court was directed towards this centre in 659, the emperor already knew about the Ashoka legend, since he quotes from it, according to reports in a

Buddhist encyclopaedia of 668. A relic was subsequently recovered at the spot, and brought to the palace to join the Buddha's skull bone that has been mentioned as an import from India; when it was returned to its place in 662 lavish donations accompanied it, including a fine scarlet robe belonging to the empress, which was recovered with other treasures by archaeologists at the site in 1987.[14]

The same encyclopaedia indicates that another cult centre, this time close to an area particularly associated with the family of the empress, also began to spark the interest of the imperial couple in 661. This one had likewise attracted the attention of earlier regimes in the area for yet longer, going back into the fifth century, but now gained added significance as the Tang dynasty sought to establish itself as an influential power in Asia as a whole. For it was alleged that this misty holy land up in the mountains was the dwelling place of none other than Manjushri, bodhisattva of wisdom, a spiritual being scarcely less numinous than the long-departed Buddha himself. Once the world knew that the great Manjushri had chosen China as his dwelling, it would surely be these mountains, and not the empty memorials to the Buddha's distantly remembered career in India, that would form the centre of the Buddhist world.[15] The spectacular long-term success of imperially sponsored information campaigns to this effect is attested by the fact that the Wutai mountains, the area in question, remain an important place of Buddhist pilgrimage (including international pilgrimage) to this day.

With both emperor and empress now engaged together in religious activities on behalf of the dynasty, it became clear that they were working as a team; they liked to be known as the 'two sages', a term used in political contexts normally of the emperor alone. Such an arrangement was not entirely unprecedented, since the founder of the preceding dynasty who had succeeded in reunifying China also explicitly shared the burden of his unaccustomed responsibilities with his empress. The clans of the north-west, with their admixture of customs derived from tough, Inner Asian warrior societies, did not discourage capable and independent women as much as one might expect. Nor were Buddhist ventures the particular sphere of the empress, for as measures relating to the fusion of Taoism and older traditional observances were developed, both sages seem to have played their part too, and where tradition limited the role of women (for example in the great sacrifices carried out on Mount Tai, the eastern holy mountain, in 666) the empress made sure that tradition was modified to give her at least some part in proceedings. In part this dual monarchy was perhaps the result not of choice on the emperor's part but of circumstance, since from quite early on in his reign he seems to have suffered from periods of ill health, including eventually what appears to have been a stroke of some sort, so that his physical capacity for meeting the executive demands of monarchy was probably limited, and he was grateful no doubt to be able to share the burdens of office for practical as well as any psychological reasons. It may well be that, ideological motives apart, some of his religious activities were intended to secure the one blessing of good health that constantly eluded him.

In his planning of the glorification of the dynastic line, however, he displayed a consistent intelligence which suggests that right up to the end of his life he was thinking ahead. In 674, for example, he proclaimed new titles for the two of them, with his particularly redolent of a Taoist Golden Age of primal kingship, while hers, Queen of Heaven, may also be found (though less conspicuously) in Taoist texts.[16] These titles did not indicate any diminution in their Buddhist interests: in 677 ten thousand relics, in convenient granular form, were discovered in a part of their capital and in the following year distributed in Ashokan fashion to every prefecture of the empire – and, it would seem, overseas – in groups of forty-nine apiece.[17] In general, the two sages seem to have promoted harmony between Buddhism and Taoism, which in crucial areas relating to the power of words overlapped in their attitudes. True, Taoism did not articulate the idea explicit in Buddhism by this time that the various 'scrolls of the scriptures are dharma-body relics', but one alchemical author addressing the emperor (and no doubt his spouse) makes it clear that at least one Taoist writer accepted the talismanic value of holy books not only of his tradition but of Buddhism as well.[18] A few years later, however, it was all over for the joint monarchy when the emperor, having survived against the odds to an even greater age than his father, finally succumbed to mortality at the end of 683.

His death can hardly have come as a surprise to the Empress Dowager (as she now became), and it must be assumed that she had long before planned to protect her position against the many enemies she had accumulated over the course of the reign. She simply switched to ruling with and for her husband to ruling through her son, who succeeded him. When he immediately showed signs of independence, she replaced him nominally with his more pliable brother, and started to promote her own relatives. But in effectively ruling solo from this point on she seems always to have been careful to build on her late husband's legacy, for example in relation to carrying out sacrifices to the god of Songshan, China's central holy mountain. This is best known today as the site of the Shaolin Monastery, home of contemporary martial arts, but it would seem that late in her husband's life he had become increasingly obsessed with carrying out the sacrifices he had already performed in 665 on the eastern holy mountain at that new location, which had never in past ages been associated with such observances. Since the holy mountains of the four cardinal directions and the centre were deemed to hold sway over certain birth years, it is my own belief, as I have stated above, that the emperor's behaviour (and hers) may have been prompted by an astrologically based desire to appease the gods that governed their lives.[19]

Other explanations of their behaviour are, however, possible.[20] Songshan is in the region of Luoyang, which had risen to prominence again as the eastern capital, as opposed to Chang'an (present-day Xi'an), further west. But in 684 it was promoted to Holy Capital, and became the centre of the empress' operations – some said because she felt that her Chang'an palace was still haunted by the ghosts of the rivals she had done to death. Even if this forms part of the explanation of her move, it seems that one of her overriding concerns from now on was to make China the centre of the world, and to situate herself at the centre of China, so that ritually everything revolved around her alone. In pursuing this aim she appears to have had in mind an intervention in history as decisive and powerful as that of the First Emperor. Reform of the Chinese script was, for example, one of her innovations, even if the reform was limited to less than a couple of dozen characters and seems to have had a rather patchy impact.[21] But she also intervened in the world of text in other ways, for example in promoting the centrality of the Wutai mountains within the Buddhist world by means of the dissemination of a new key translation of a Buddhist text, based on a particularly powerful 'spell'; it may be significant that this 'spell' is personified in Indo-Tibetan Buddhism (though somewhat rarely in East Asia) as a female figure.[22] This work was allegedly brought from India at Manjushri's explicit command by an Indian monk who had encountered the great bodhisattva on the Wutai mountains, expressly because of the benefits it could bring China: if inscribed on an octagonal pillar, the very shadow of the text, or a very mote of dust falling from its surface, could cancel out vast quantities of bad karma for any individual who came into contact with it. Nothing could be more effective as a means of producing physically solid and reassuring objects in their way equivalent to Buddha relics that could calm a population nervous about the inevitable decline of Buddhism, and these pillars (many of which survive) soon started to spread across the land. By 813 at the latest, as is recorded in an inscription of that date, people were taking rubbings from the pillars and distributing them, so that this work became amongst the first in history known to have benefited from mechanical reproduction, even if the sheets more than a metre high taken from the incised surfaces did not have the convenience of either the scroll or codex form.[23] Before turning to look further at the contributions to printing made by the empress, however, it is necessary to make a few additional points about the development of her career.

Remaining a mere Empress Dowager was far from the height of her ambitions. In general one of the great advantages of following her husband's line in developing an ideology of imperial rule based on Taoist symbolism was that the Chinese religion is perhaps one of the least patriarchal of the world's major faiths – images of the female are prominent in the *Daode jing*, and Taoist goddesses and priestesses playing prominent roles are easy to find in medieval sources. By the middle of 688 a carefully orchestrated campaign of prophecy – still visible under later layers of rather different rhetoric in documents associated with her rule – culminated in her assumption of a new title, 'Sage Mother, Holy Sovereign'. Even so, it must have been extremely galling to her to be a Sage Mother, in that it was only her Li family sons that made her so, and several members of the family had already expressed their feelings about her by rising in armed rebellion at the start of her solo rule. In the interim she had taken up with a Buddhist lover, the distinctly Rasputinesque cult leader mentioned in the opening chapter, who no doubt put her in touch with the pulse of popular belief but who was himself violently anti-Taoist. One can imagine the fervour with which learned Buddhists must have ransacked their scriptures, looking for their own prophecies of female rule. In the nick of time they succeeded, though the prophecy in the original text referred plainly to south India, not China, and some very learned commentary was required to make it clear that the Sage Mother was in fact the person to whom the prediction applied. In 690, with no need to be beholden to the Li family any more, she declared her own dynasty, with herself as emperor, knowing that any die-hard traditionalists were by this point unlikely to have escaped the past attentions of her secret police. These most unpleasant servants of her rule had been active ever since the Li family first opposed her, and in the wake of another rebellion prompted by her incipient moves to Sage Mother status had been thorough in weeding out dissent. Of her forty-six chief ministers between 684 and 693, for example, it has been calculated that half suffered a violent end to their life through suicide or execution, and three-quarters had their careers suddenly terminated either by such violent deaths or by exile.[24]

From 690 onwards, then, until her eventual deposition early in 705, her power was supreme: her sons lived, but the erstwhile puppet emperor was forced to change his family name to hers. Her own blood relatives were also kept in order, and her Buddhist Rasputin was, as has already been noted, eventually beaten to death at her command. Meanwhile, she abandoned her career as a Sage Mother and awarded herself instead a series of more Buddhist titles, usually including the words 'Chakravartin of the Golden Wheel' and briefly claiming that she was simultaneously Maitreya, Buddha of the Future, as well. In short, her image amongst the population at large (who escaped more or less unscathed from the attentions of the secret police) remained a matter of concern to her, and it is important to remember this in the next chapter which examines her later years and what they have to tell us about the emergence of printing.

CHAPTER SIX

A WOMAN ALONE

Before any discussion of the part that her religious ideology may have played in promoting the development of printing, it is worth noting that the woman whose career has been traced in the preceding chapter is already in the history books – at least in China – for her use of printed materials in a purely secular context.[1] So even if the hypotheses advanced in the rest of this chapter are not accepted, it is undeniable that this woman discovered printing in the sense that she found a use in imperial administration for written materials produced by mechanical reproduction, though these were only small items produced by stamping, rather than taken from larger blocks. In a work of the early ninth century, and again in an eleventh-century history that was based on a now lost official historiography going back almost a century earlier than that, are reports of a story dated to 691, soon after her accession as emperor. At that time it was widely surmised that she wished to replace the Li imperial line permanently with her own relatives, and some sought to curry favour with her by suggesting a new heir apparent from within her family. One zealous proponent of the idea was so earnest that, in order to get rid of him, she gave him a security pass to allow him back into the palace to see her whenever he wanted. He seems to have had little conception of how dangerous a world he had entered, for by abusing this privilege he incurred her displeasure, with the consequence that her agents swiftly took him away and beat him to death.[2]

The security pass is given in both surviving sources as a *yinzhi*, literally meaning a 'seal-paper', evidently a document consisting of a piece of paper stamped with a seal. The term does occur earlier, in a religious work generally dated to the sixth century, which was amongst the texts on the use of seals studied by Michel Strickmann. In that context, however, the 'seal-paper' is never read (by humans at any rate), but always swallowed or burned to ashes in order to accomplish some magical purpose.[3] So although it is possible to say that if the date of this work is correct, the use of stamped text on its own rather than as an addition to some other document probably preceded the stamping of images as creations in their own right by the Taoists, it was not until 691 that scholars can be sure that such stamped products achieved anything more than a highly ephemeral existence. And there is one other indication that under the reign of China's only female emperor seals had been reconceptualised so that they were not thought of simply as added markers of authority but more as matrices for the creation of new documents. A late source suggests that under her rule so many new appointments were made that her seal-carvers gave up making individual seals and instead produced pro forma stamps to which a written signature had to be added.[4]

It is also possible that a similar evolution in the understanding of the seal had taken place by this time in some religious circles, but the evidence is not dated exactly. In the early tenth century an account of a line of hereditary Taoist masters said to stretch back to the Han dynasty notes that in the thirteenth generation the masters began to 'manufacture on paper' (to quote our source) talismanic documents formerly carved into wood. The fifteenth master in this lineage seems to have lived in the middle of the eighth century, so it would be reasonable to place his predecessor's predecessor in the late seventh. If the wooden talisman had actually served as seals, then it would seem that the rising popularity of the cult had again caused a change in tactics, and that as with the case of the overworked imperial seal-carvers, this was prompted by an imbalance between supply and demand.[5]

But although (as we shall see) this is not the only evidence for Taoist printing at this time, it is by a comparison of what has already been noted in Taoism with a Buddhist source that something rather interesting emerges – something which suggests that the Chakravartin of the Golden Wheel had plans to enhance her Buddhist image in which the multiple mechanical reproduction of powerful texts perhaps played some part.

The passage in question may be found in the writings of a monk who travelled across Asia for over twenty years, from 671 to 693, to learn more about Buddhism. The heroic Buddhist traveller who had gone to India in the time of the old emperor was in fact neither the first nor the last of his brethren to succeed in visiting the places where the Buddha had taught and in bringing back more scriptures to translate, though few indeed survived the journey both ways, and fewer still were fortunate enough to return to a Chinese regime prepared to furnish the resources that a large translation team needed. The reputation of this particularly intrepid and lucky traveller has in the popular imagination completely overshadowed that of the next great Chinese pilgrim to India, Yijing (635–713), a man who not only returned to translate a respectably large quantity of materials into Chinese but also made his own contribution to our knowledge of South Asia at this time that is today just as valuable as the travel account bequeathed by his predecessor. For rather than describe the route of his journeys, he wrote a more discursive description of Buddhist practice in India and in the 'Indianised' states of South-East Asia at the time. Of course this description was not in any sense a matter of unbiased anthropological observation.

Yijing had his own ideas about the way in which the Buddhist clergy in China fell short, and no doubt took pains to address the problems he perceived.[6] Modern scholarship has noted that what appears to be eyewitness material is actually translated from texts on Buddhist canon law, and although Yijing spoke to a number of fellow Chinese pilgrims who took the transcontinental route to India, he himself came and went by sea, so those passages relating to Tibetan customs and so forth cannot be direct eyewitness evidence either.

We also know that, at the time of composing his description of South Asia, Yijing was well informed concerning events in China, since during the four years he spent on writing up his observations he was living not in India but in Sumatra, far closer by ship to China on a much used trading route. At one point, moreover, he tells us that in an effort to replenish his supplies of Chinese ink and paper he went on board a merchant vessel trading between there and present-day Canton and was accidentally carried off back to his homeland, only returning to Sumatra after three months. This suspicious-looking 'accident' meant that as he wrote up his final version of the text with all the authority of residence in what was not simply a foreign but also a Buddhist country, he would have been very well informed about the religious and political climate in China at the time the Tang dynasty was supplanted by the Zhou dynasty. Indeed, since he did not reappear at the Holy Capital from south China until 695, he would have had ample opportunity to tailor his remarks to his intended imperial audience, as the final words of his text praising the Zhou dynasty attest. In the same year he also played an important part in authenticating a jade tablet inscribed with mysterious writing and 'discovered' in a stone chest; presumably drawing on his fame as a master of foreign languages he pronounced it a divine endorsement of the rule of the Sage Mother, as she still was. It was this auspicious omen, so it is said, which prompted her to change her title to that of Chakravartin.[7] All the indications are, in fact, that from some time before this episode he had been a close ideological collaborator with some of the key Buddhist supporters of the new regime.[8]

Now at one point in his description of South Asian Buddhist life, Yijing tells us about how images of the Buddha were made, and amongst these he includes the making of Buddhist snowmen. He cannot have witnessed this himself, since his travels in India were confined to the hotter plains, nor is there any reference to making snowmen in any of the texts of Buddhist canon law that he himself later translated; indeed, there are only one or two slight references to snowmen in any of the Buddhist literature translated before or after his time, and nothing to show independently that snow Buddhas were an accepted part of religious practice in South Asia. But it is known from the text discussed in Chapter Four that snow images were part of seventh-century Taoism, and one cannot help but suspect that this passage may have been inserted by Yijing to help his co-religionists in their competition with their rivals by endorsing the legitimacy of using the same image-producing techniques. So what is one to make of the assertion in the same passage that images were also made by stamping on silk, or on paper? Silk at this point in South Asian history was an import from China, and paper too was as rare in India as it evidently was by Yijing's own account in Sumatra, so once again the comparison with the earlier Taoist text suggests that this too is an addition that he made with the Chinese situation in mind.

The passage then moves on to mention the use of the Buddhist doctrinal formula to constitute a relic in written form, a practice which is certainly authentically Indian, as was seen in Chapter Four. Given what we have already learned about his ruler's interest in relics, might it be that she needed in particular to know that textual relics stamped on to paper – something not explicitly mentioned by Yijing but justifiable on the basis of his remarks – could be a useful technology for a Chinese Ashoka? At first glance there is nothing to suggest that she was dissatisfied with existing methods of disseminating texts: there even exist today copies of the *Lotus Sutra* in manuscript deriving from a set of three thousand made for the posthumous karmic benefit of her parents, an enterprise that would have involved the creation of 21,000 scrolls.[9] For a son who died – probably of natural causes, though her detractors of course suspect poison – she had had copied out at least one set of the entire Taoist scriptures, in about two thousand scrolls, and perhaps many times that figure.[10] Even more amazingly, a chance reference concerning the mid-ninth century reveals that she had five thousand scrolls of Buddhist scriptures recreated in embroidery.[11] Anyone prepared to underwrite such a venture was evidently not too interested in the economics of publishing.

There is no question but that playing Ashoka would have been a relatively easy task for her. Producing ten thousand relics in non-textual form in 677 seems to have posed no problem, and Yijing had actually brought one hundred more back from India since then. But if 84,000 jewel-like objects were more than she could easily lay her hands on, producing 84,000 short manuscripts to substitute for them would surely have been well within the capacity of her copyists. Unfortunately, she appears to have vowed to distribute getting on for one hundred times that figure, so however lavish her patronage of more conventional methods of copying, she would surely have considered the use of mechanical means of producing texts, and at least conducted a few prudent experiments.[12] It is true that there is no contemporary source that mentions the use of wooden blocks, while for anything longer than the sort of short doctrinal formula used in India a block rather than a stamp would have been necessary. But some Chinese scholars believe that in one or two cases printed copies of short spells written in Sanskrit retrieved from tombs – the use of this type of text in funerary observances in India has already been mentioned – actually date to before her time.[13] Be that as it may, the practice of taking rubbings from inscriptions – the imperial palace included a small team of experts permanently employed in such work – plus the mention of Gong Xuanxuan and his jade 'printing block' as early as the fifth century, lead one to believe that employing small woodblocks would not have been beyond the imagination of her artisans.

But perhaps it was neither the cheapness of woodblock printing nor the high volume of copies it made possible that attracted the Chakravartin of the Golden Wheel so much as the speed with which they could be produced. To boast of a vow to make hundreds of thousands of reliquaries might have been all right as part of the virtuosic manipulation of symbols and portents that preceded the declaration of her own dynasty, but how did it look as the dynasty entered its second decade, and she grew older and increasingly tired? Or so it would seem, from the fact that towards the end of her reign she had retreated from involvement in day-to-day administration in favour of spending more and more time with some amusing and beautiful young male favourites. Or was she too disengaged in the end to bother about ideology at all? With most remote elderly and powerful autocrats in history one would love to know how far they believed in their own image – what one might call the Ozymandias syndrome – and how far they thought otherwise. Until about seven o'clock in the evening of 21 May 1982, she was among this number, but since then scholars have had solid evidence as to where her most heartfelt and private concerns lay. It was at this time that an agricultural worker named Qu Xihuai, coming to the end of a day of tree planting high on the slopes of Songshan, noticed under a large rock first a coin, and then a longer, flatter object, which gleamed when he rubbed the mud off it. This turned out to be a slip of gold, on which was written a message from Wu Zhao (as she referred to herself, using her straightforward family and personal names alone), ruler of the land of the Great Zhou, as she called her own personal dynasty, to the gods of Taoism (cf. Note on Transcription and Sources, above).[14]

The discovery of such a message is by no means unique: similar inscriptions on slips of gold have been retrieved from other mountains, and from lakes. They derive from the medieval Taoist ritual of 'hurling dragons', in which an inscribed message to the gods was attached to a metal model of a dragon and hurled into space, either to vanish into the misty mountain air or sink under the waters. Rulers would frequently have their agents carry out these rituals, which they normally declared to be conducted not simply in their own interest but also on behalf of their entire polity, to ask for general blessings such as good harvests.[15] Other surviving examples do not always bear out these protestations of public-spiritedness, and this one certainly does not. Of the sixty-three characters of text, twenty-four are taken up with the date (27 July 700, when converted to the Julian calendar) and the name of the officiating priest.[16] I have already given the author's name, as it appears on the slip; the remaining core of the message consists of thirty-one characters, which translate as follows: 'Loving the true Way and the long-living holy immortals, I have respectfully come to the mountain gate of the Central Peak, Song the lofty, and cast one golden slip, begging the three palaces and nine departments to erase the wrongdoing name of Wu Zhao.' Translating the religious ideas embodied in this plea involves some compromises: 'immortals' are not always literally immortal, and 'wrongdoings' is a way of avoiding the word 'sins', which would tend to presuppose a Christian context. The three palaces and nine departments administer the world of the dead, on the basis of files recording their misdeeds; medieval Chinese would resort to any means (including identity theft) to try to placate this inexorable bureaucracy.[17] So the woman who had murdered her way to the top and terrorised her high officials was not a completely amoral psychopath after all: in this purely private message, perhaps known only to the priest who inscribed it while on the mountain, she shows that she was conscious of the possible spiritual consequences of her actions, and anxious to set matters straight before she had to account for herself in another world.

But if this solid gold document and other inscriptions on stone from other mountains suggest that the Chakravartin of the Golden Wheel, for all her use of Buddhist ideas in her ideology, continued to sustain a private commitment to Taoism, it might be unwise to conclude that her interest in Buddhism was merely a matter for public consumption. She evidently paid special attention to the new translations of texts incorporating powerful spells that became available during her reign, including one that advertised its potency

THE CENTRALITY OF SONGSHAN, I
3. A map of the area produced for a local publication of 1984 as a reconstruction of an original of 1529.

4. A monochrome image of the dragon's message, created from a modern facsimile of the golden tablet.

within a stupa as 100,000 times greater than an ordinary scripture, while another such text was honoured by her with dissemination in embroidered form. But there was one collection of spells above all that appears to have seized her imagination in her final years, as bouts of illness warned her that her life as a Chakravartin was drawing to its close. It is not just that this text offered (as others did) more years to the life of one who produced copies of it, nor yet that it guaranteed rebirth in a paradise to any deceased persons who had multiple copies made on their behalf. Michael E. Welch, in an unpublished study completed over a quarter of a century ago, noted that the title of the work, *Great Spell of Unsullied Pure Light,* would have suggested to her a connection with the future female ruler of Buddhist prophecy, the goddess Pure Light, with whom her monkish supporters had identified her in order to make her new dynasty possible in 690.[18] This work, well known in India as an adjunct to funerary practices, was first translated by a Khotanese monk and then retranslated by a Tokharian, together with a Chinese Buddhist of Sogdian descent, not long before 705.[19] In the middle of that year a group of Tang loyalists, exasperated by her indulgence of her favourites, deposed her in a coup, though her eventual death before the year was out seems to have been due to entirely natural causes.

But it is what happened next to the *Great Spell of Unsullied Pure Light* that has caused several scholars to wonder independently about the old Great Sage Dowager Empress Zetian (as she became at her end, renouncing all her other imperial titles) and the emergence of printing. By the middle of 706, to judge from an inscription, it had arrived in Korea, since a lost copy was at that date placed in a royal reliquary by a king who does not mind telling us that he was seeking to prolong his life. By 751 (according to most Korean scholars, though the matter is hotly contested) someone had placed another, surviving printed copy in a Korean stupa, whence it was recovered in 1966, making it quite possibly the oldest printed document in the world. And, incontestably, between 764 and 770 a Japanese empress distributed a million small wooden stupas containing spells excerpted from the text – the historical record aside, so many actual examples survive to this day that no one has any trouble in believing that she probably achieved her goal, or at least came remarkably close.[20] It is surely not a coincidence that one finds the *Great Spell of Unsullied Pure Light* not simply associated with a funerary context as in India, but with monarchy in both Korea and Japan – an association not attested for India to my knowledge – and quite specifically in the latter case with an Ashokan form of monarchy featuring the distribution of relics.

Here was a pattern in which the private desire of monarchs for longevity or a good rebirth could combine with a public act stressing the Buddhist credentials of their rule. The parallel with the dual nature of the dragon-hurling ceremony, in which public prayers for national prosperity turn out to have provided a private opportunity to petition the gods, surely reflects the approach of China's only female emperor, the Chakravartin of the Golden Wheel, in its subtle combination of the careful nurturing of a public image amongst the masses and ruthless self-interest. If we wish to regard printing as an independent invention in Korea or (if we discount the Korean evidence) in Japan, then we must also regard this pattern as an independent invention. The sole point that prevents us from attributing this earliest physical evidence for printing to an emulation of her earlier example is the lack of any transmitted source or archaeologically recovered printed document making clear her role in the matter.

Perhaps the latter will one day surface, or perhaps very early printed material exhibiting the modified characters she introduced will be shown to derive from her reign.[21] But the lack of reference to woodblock printing activity on her part in any transmitted Chinese source is hardly surprising. After her death the son who had originally opposed her wishes once more ascended the throne. Next, after this man's wife (who does seem to have modelled herself on her mother-in-law, though she lacked her finesse) poisoned him, his pliable brother was also brought back, until further infighting resulted in the emergence of a grandson – a younger, more dynamic emperor who restored the Li family fortunes. In name the Zhou dynasty of Wu Zetian perished with her forced abdication, and the Tang dynasty after a few years of instability continued – if not without problems – for another two centuries. Her usurpation of the divinely descended Lis, even if she had believed in their status enough not to extirpate them, was enough to make her and all her works anathema to the regime, and even when in time it changed, the general prejudice against powerful women ensured her a negative historical press from all but a few iconoclasts. It is not simply that were it not for the 1982 discovery on Songshan little would be known of her inner thoughts: her public acts, too, were deliberately edited from the record in many instances, leaving only occasional traces of the rewriting of history. A few items of useful information can still be gleaned from transmitted materials, especially religious ones: it is possible to discern, for example, from a preface to a Buddhist translation she composed in 700 that her interest in the

Ashokan distribution of relics did not fade in her later years.[22] But it is not just the Songshan discovery of 1982 that has allowed us to fill in a little bit more of some tantalising gaps only in comparatively recent times: the entire document whereby her monkish commentators proved that the south Indian goddess Pure Light had actually appeared in China was lost to historians until it was discovered amongst the Dunhuang manuscripts in the early twentieth century. Perhaps one day newly unearthed inscriptions will enable us to take the story further.

For now, however, there are two more lines of inquiry that can be pursued to try to get to the truth of what exactly happened to the *Great Spell of Unsullied Pure Light* in China. One so far has got me nowhere, and that is the study of later relic distributions in China. If one could point to a distribution of relics in imitation of Ashoka that used printed texts in China independently of the events known to have taken place in Japan, then that would argue strongly that they both derived from some anterior precedent, and the Chakravartin of the Golden Wheel would be a prime candidate for having provided a model in both cases. In the tenth century a king who ruled in the lower Yangzi region is known from transmitted and archaeological evidence to have used printed spells inserted into quite elaborate stupas, which were distributed not only across his own domains but also overseas. The text concerned was not, however, the *Great Spell of Unsullied Pure Light* but a similar work translated several decades later, and we cannot be sure that he was drawing on any Chinese precedent, since his overseas contacts included good relations with both Japan and Korea.[23] If indeed we look for indications of any precedent in China between his time and the year 705, then even the emperor best placed to have played Ashoka, who lived in the middle of the ninth century, seems to have done nothing of the sort.[24] Some of the later members of the Li family were inclined towards Buddhism, and did not always rest on the credentials provided for them by divine descent, but none apparently wished to do anything to remind their subjects of the hated female usurper.

The closest parallel from mainland East Asia, and one that is independent of both the Japanese example and indeed of the influence of the king of the lower Yangzi, may be found in the actions of the rulers of the Tanguts, whose prowess as twelfth-century masters of movable type printing will be recalled from Chapter One. The Ashokan ideal of Buddhist kingship was important to Tangut rulers, and at least one of them was a great distributor of Buddhist texts and images.[25] We know from archaeology too that the Tanguts were great producers of miniature stupas, into some of which they inserted textual materials in manuscript or print.[26] Unfortunately, however, so far I know of no explicit link between the two, no exact parallel to the Ashokan distribution of stupas with printed materials inside, though since at the moment only a handful of people across the globe can read the Tangut language there is undoubtedly much more to learn about their history.

But there remains one more body of information to discuss. Though the artisans who would have carved the Chakravartin of the Golden Wheel's woodblocks, if there were any, are most unlikely to have left any trace in the historical record, the project was probably not under the direct supervision of the old woman herself. That is why I have imagined the Venerable Bede discerning another figure in her presence, a Buddhist holy man. Again, several scholars have come up with an educated guess as to which Buddhist amongst her entourage this would have been, and the time has come to consider the evidence for his involvement. Yijing was still alive at this time, but the most likely candidate is another man to whom brief allusion has already been made in passing. He is so important, however, that he deserves some extended discussion in his own right, even if, as pointed out in the Introduction, my study is now obliged to turn from the explanation of the ideas behind religious printing to investigation of some quite recondite details in the next two chapters. If these investigations do not at first seem conclusive, then I must beg the reader's patience: the final chapter will make use of the evidence reviewed in detail to suggest broader lines of interpretation.

CHAPTER SEVEN

OF MONKS AND MYSTERIES

If Bede had really seen the man in front of the great female monarch in faraway China, his shaven head would probably have suggested his religious status to his English contemporary. But Bede would no doubt have noticed too that his face suggested a rather different ethnic background from the woman at the centre of the scene. Fazang (643–712) was the Buddhist of Sogdian descent who helped to translate the earliest dated piece of printing now in existence, the *Great Spell of Unsullied Light*. The Sogdians were an Iranian people dwelling in the region of present-day Samarkand on the eastern borders of the civilisation of Iran. They had long been traders, by sea and land, right across Asia, and China had for centuries been one of their most important destinations. At this time many of them (in China, at least) were Buddhists, too, capable of putting their great wealth and wide range of business contacts at the service of the Buddhist clergy. Apparently, however, Fazang's grandfather, a prominent member of Samarkand's political elite, had come to China on a diplomatic mission and decided to stay, so that Fazang was born in China, probably in the capital, where his father held a minor post in the imperial palace guards.[1]

Fazang's religious life seems to have been destined even from his adolescence to bring him into contact with his ruler. As early as 658 he is said to have shown his commitment to Buddhism by sacrificing one of his own fingers – a dramatic but not unparalleled form of Buddhist piety – at the very shrine that was to attract the attention of the emperor and his wife to the legend of Ashoka and his heroic feats of relic distribution in the following year, as was mentioned in Chapter Five. But at first the young zealot shunned court life, preferring to devote himself to one of the most abstruse new trends in Buddhist thought to have emerged from the religious ferment of the late sixth century. Many of these new trends can be seen as attempting in a world fraught with uncertainty to find the meaning of Buddhism in the here and now, rather than to cling to memories of the Buddha's teachings long ago and far away in India. Those scriptures that had established themselves not simply as relics of the Buddha but as part of Chinese everyday religious life were particularly carefully read for clues as to how they might help make sense of life as experienced during the dramatic events of the sixth and seventh centuries.

Among interpreters of these texts Fazang was most attracted to those who, in the light of their own experience of meditation, were propounding a new way of looking at the *Huayan Scripture*. This is a massive work that was thought to embody the very content of the Buddha's enlightenment, which none of his human listeners could fathom until the Buddha had decided for pedagogical reasons to go back to basics and spend years teaching more simple doctrines. As further interpreted in China, therefore, it does not lend itself to easy summary, and Fazang's achievement in mastering and commenting on what he perceived to be its major doctrines has earned him a reputation as one of the most erudite and sophisticated of all East Asian Buddhist thinkers. If one were, however, to venture a summary of one of its key insights against the background of the insecure and fearful age that has been described above, then it would be that all reality is interconnected through and through, down to (as we would say in the twenty-first century) the smallest particle and the shortest instant, so that in each of these the totality of the rest of existence is reflected. But it would be a mistake to see this vision of reality as simply a topic for the philosophically inclined to ponder, for one corollary of this way of looking at the world to those who managed through religious disciplining of their mind to achieve some mastery of it would be the reassurance that time and space do not divide us from enlightenment. Far from having to worry about the life of the Buddha having been so far away and long ago, enlightenment turns out to be part of the structure of the universe all sentient beings inhabit here and now, if only they have eyes to see it. And, seen or unseen, at the highest level of reality, encompassing the whole, is an ultimate, cosmic Buddha personified under the name Vairocana.

One wonders if it was this picture of a dizzying level of ultimate power personified that first attracted the attention of China's only female ruler to the studies of the young philosopher; certainly the lofty image of Vairocana that she subsequently had carved into the riverside cliffs not far from her Holy Capital still has the power to impress, and perhaps even to reconnect us to her own notions of imperial rule, for all the time and space that lie between her and us. In any case, in 670, on the death of her mother, she seems to have ordered that Fazang should be given a tonsure, to make him a member of the clergy, and assigned him to the new monastery converted from her late parent's former dwelling; like a number of clerics of the age, he seems to have been satisfied with novice status, since there is no early source to show that he ever proceeded to full ordination. Thereafter until the end of her reign he was frequently employed to give lectures on the worldview of the *Huayan Scripture,* to help translate the new materials containing the Buddha's word that reached China under her regime, and generally to use his numinous presence to support her through such religious and yet to the contemporary mind practical activities as rainmaking ceremonies or confounding foreign armies with his magic.

Fazang, for all his superior intellectual reputation, was not merely a philosopher, but also a practical and extremely shrewd man, who knew about a surprising variety of things. It has recently been pointed out, for example, that the manufacture of the distinctive paper made from mulberry bark that was used in the Korean printing of the *Great Spell of Unsullied Light* is referred to a couple of times in his surviving writings.[2] He is probably best known for arranging for his imperial patron a display of reflecting mirrors, to give her some idea of the worldview that he found in his texts, though this mastery of optical technology was not too unusual in his day. Bedchambers full of mirrors were built for some of the debauched predecessors to the Li imperial line, and Buddhist monks had already adapted the underlying idea to the more salubrious purpose of explaining their view of the universe. Nor did Buddhist knowledge focus on metaphor alone: a study of surviving Buddhist art and architecture of the period reveals that an understanding of optics was part of the technological know-how that Buddhists used in their reproduction of images.[3] Professor J. Sugiyama of the International College of Advanced Buddhist Studies in Tokyo has gone even further in linking Fazang to the Buddhist art of the day in suggesting the specific influence of Fazang's ideas about Vairocana on the iconography of the temple built by his patron in the final years of her reign to celebrate the hoard of relics discovered earlier in 677.[4]

Interestingly, Professor Sugiyama also sees the same influence in the iconography of some stamped clay tiles from the famous Great Goose pagoda that still stands in Xi'an. This was erected in 652, but it is known that it was repaired late in her reign. But if these tiles do reflect Fazang's influence, then their actual manufacture must relate to a late stage of refurbishment after her removal, since what he takes as a stamped inscription on them refers to the dynasty as the

'Great Tang', rather than the 'Great Zhou', as would have been the case under her rule. The full inscription given by Sugiyama is intriguing. It reads 'Great Tang good karma clay, pressed into the body of the wonderful likeness of True Suchness.' 'Good karma clay' is a phrase taken by scholars to indicate that the cremated ashes of holy people – and perhaps, indeed, of ordinary people who wished their remains to become part of a holy place – had been mixed with clay to form holy relics.[5] The 'body of the wonderful likeness' is another Buddhist phrase, particularly common in the *Huayan Scripture,* while 'True Suchness' translates a term for the Absolute, the ultimate level of reality personified by Vairocana. Each tile, then, with its Buddha image and perhaps as a result of its holy clay constituents too, formed a miniature relic in itself and, if Fazang was involved, the possible use of stamped text on these relics is especially interesting.

Also significant is the clustering of this activity in the final years of the life of the rapidly ageing Chakravartin of the Golden Wheel. Even were it not for the discovery of her secret prayer to the Taoist gods that reveals the degree of her preoccupation with the world beyond, the historical record shows well enough that during this period her health gave her frequent grounds for concern. About a year before her death, the situation was evidently so bad that Fazang was sent to fetch the finger bone relic in front of which he had sacrificed his own finger all those years ago, and bring it to her in the Holy Capital, in the hope that its miraculous powers would give her strength. But relics, it seems, move in mysterious ways, for not a week had passed after Fazang brought the holy object to her than she was Chakravartin no more: her favourites had been executed, and she had been deposed. Furthermore, if the careful detective work of Jinhua Chen is correct, Fazang had switched sides.[6] If he had started the week believing that the talisman of his zealous youth would cure his patron it must have been a taxing seven days, and when she did eventually die, less than nine months later, both he

AT THE END OF HER DAYS
5. An April 2007 photograph of the famous tombstone with nothing written on it – taken from the back, since writing was eventually added to the front in later ages.

6. A listing of the *Great Spell* in a later bibliography of the Buddhist Canon, printed in the seventeenth century.

金剛祕密善門陀羅尼呪經

右三經本同譯別說此呪能保祐眾生有種種持

法

無垢淨光大陀羅尼經

右婆羅門七日當命終墮大地獄禮佛求救佛爲

說此延壽滅罪陀羅尼令修古佛舍利壞塔安此

陀羅尼于輪橖中供養得延壽滅罪有種種儀法

橖塔中柱也及造塔當檢用

請觀世音消伏毒害陀羅尼經

右說陀羅尼能護救一切眾生消伏毒害種種障難

內藏百寶經

右說佛方便智隨順世間諸示現事

and the new regime he now supported would have been left in an awkward situation. For if belief in the spirit world meant anything, then an immensely powerful spirit unafraid of causing pain and death on a considerable scale, apparently without compunction, had just arrived among the ranks of the unseen.[7]

The political climate was nothing if not tricky, with stability almost a decade away, so that any decision as to how to deal posthumously with the most anomalous ruler in Chinese history must have been a headache for all concerned – perhaps this may explain why although a memorial stone was prepared for her, all divided off into neat squares for the characters to be incised within, nobody during the life of the dynasty ever got round to carving an inscription on it.[8] Chinese funeral rites, too, were and are not simply a matter of a single day: those of deceased imperial persons involved quite lengthy and extended rituals. There is no record of the relevant official rituals – which in any case paid no attention to specifically Buddhist or Taoist observances – until 779, but at this time they took seven months from death to burial, so whatever ritual moves were set in motion late in 705 would have continued right up to the assignment of the late empress to her final resting place, well into 706.[9] In that year – at the beginning of June, according to the histories – she ended up once more beside her husband in the massive mausoleum that had already been provided for him. Meanwhile the reburial of various members of the Li family to whom she had not given their due at the times of their deaths – quite besides any refurbishment of her husband's mausoleum required for her own burial – had entailed simultaneous building work on an extended scale, so the government would have been preoccupied with considerable ritual and (yet more onerously) construction activity.[10] What might Fazang have done during this crucial, politically unsettled and very busy period – in Buddhist belief, initially an especially significant time during which reincarnation would have been determined – to placate the spirit of his late patron?[11]

On the assumption that something like the scene I have imagined in Bede's revelation had indeed taken place somewhat earlier, and that the required technology was therefore tested and available, the Korean and Japanese evidence gives us a strong clue. It is not just that the distribution of the *Great Spell of Unsullied Light* as a Buddha relic in textual form would have accomplished both the private purpose of securing a good rebirth and the public one of emulating Ashoka. Relics were distributed in Japan, it should be recalled, as part of enthronement rituals, certainly to ensure the

Ashokan status of the new occupant of the throne, but perhaps also with an awareness of some function with regard to its late occupant, the new emperor's predecessor. And as soon as the *Great Spell* arrived in Korea, it was immediately put to use in the interests of both the living monarch and his deceased father, by the new king's own admission. For that matter, even if this first arrival was in manuscript, it seems to have shown up at a time (14 July 706) that followed very closely upon the funeral rites of the recently deceased ruler of the Great Zhou in China, the erstwhile Chakravartin of the Golden Wheel.[12] The scripture could of course have arrived by other means – Fazang is known to have sent some of his own writings to a Korean former fellow student in 690, and the very covering letter accompanying these gifts is believed by some to have survived.[13] One of Yijing's translations, too, seems to have arrived in Korea through diplomatic channels within half a year or so of the completion of the Chinese version in 703, a project in which Fazang was also involved, and both Chinese and Korean records note an embassy from Korea in May–June 706, perhaps not unconnected with the funerary rituals of the time.[14]

But a distribution at this time would explain the use of printing, for otherwise, were there not enough copyists in China to create the requisite quantity? In Japan, later in the century, creating a million copies of even this very short work would have been very difficult in a country where literacy (which during this period, before the invention of the Japanese script, meant literacy in Chinese) was very thinly spread. But in China it could be done, though not in a hurry. And it is known that Fazang understood the benefits of speed conveyed by alternatives to manual copying, because he comments on them explicitly twice in earlier writings.[15] In fact Buddhists seem from early on to have shown an interest in the automatic transfer of patterns through moulds and the like, since their view of the workings of the universe saw karma as automatically providing an impersonal causality driving on the constant 'Wheel of Life' through incessant reincarnations. The very mention of reincarnation to many familiar with other religious traditions would naturally spark thoughts of the existence of a soul that reincarnates from life to life. But the Buddhist view of karma would see the process as much more like that of the impersonal transfer of pattern achieved by a mould or a seal, a sort of transfer of a collection of data rather than the survival of anything like a spiritual essence of personhood. This type of image may be found both in the Mahayana literature familiar to the Chinese and in more conservative texts preserved in South Asia, so it was probably well known to all Buddhists from quite early on.[16]

But whereas Fazang would no doubt have been familiar with these metaphorical comparisons stressing the accuracy of the karmic process, he puts the imagery involved to a somewhat different use which shows that his appreciation of the factors involved in the creation of writing by automatic means encompassed other concerns as well. I have mentioned already how his view of the *Huayan Scripture* saw it as representing the very content of the Buddha's enlightenment, a doctrine so profound that the Buddha found no one capable of understanding it, obliging him to go back to basics and to teach his disciples a sequence of doctrines from the simpler to the more profound. Given that Fazang also saw the Buddha's enlightenment as something that happened at a stroke rather than as some gradually dawning apprehension, this naturally raised the question of how something could be instantaneous yet contain a sequential structure. Fazang's explanation (with my own comments in brackets) is as follows: 'All the doctrines of the Buddha were preached together on the fourteenth day [after his enlightenment] at once from beginning to end, from beginning to end at once. This is just as in this [contemporary] world, with the use of a seal; we read its text as a meaningful unit from beginning to end [we construe it sequentially]. When the text is impressed, then it appears all at the same time, yet this does not go against the principle of it having at the same time a beginning and an end [a sequential structure].' Here I have deliberately translated this passage on the by now somewhat unlikely assumption that printing (as opposed to stamping with a seal) was unknown to him, but from medieval Japan onwards many readers have assumed that the use of woodblocks to print text is what he has in mind – the word for 'seal' is used in compounds to indicate printing even today in East Asia. But even if this passage does not refer to woodblock technology as we know it – and it was plainly written earlier in his career, well before the translation of the *Great Spell* – it is still quite certain that Fazang would have understood the advantage of speed that this technology provides.

But once we admit that a passage such as the one just translated may at least have a bearing on how the process of printing might have been understood, then the religious literature produced under the Zhou dynasty and shortly thereafter reveals at least one or two other very valuable scraps of information. An eminent Taoist priest, for example, when he needs to explain how the Tao, the underlying power that is in everything, can at the same time be something distinct – the problem of unity and multiplicity – uses a metaphor revealing what might be a significant shift in contemporary thinking. It is, he says, like a seal, which can replicate a portion of text many times over and yet be unchanged. Once more our source has moved beyond the seal as the accurate conveyer of data to an object that can replicate the same words repeatedly – and if this is not a description of printing, then at least it suggests that the high volume of copies a woodblock can produce would have been fully appreciated by people at this time. Again, since this man died in 695, it is possible to be quite sure that this facet of understanding of the possibilities of mechanical reproduction antedates the translation of the *Great Spell*. As for the matter of the accuracy of seals in data transfer, stressed by Indian texts, it is just as certain that the Chinese would have understood this too, because another monk, who was incidentally a colleague of Fazang on one of the Great Zhou dynasty translation teams, uses a metaphor to this effect, independently of any Indian text, in a commentary of the period.

But quite beyond the fact that a study of religious metaphors confirms that the speed, volume and accuracy of copying provided by printing would have been well understood by religious persons of about CE 700, there is one reference that hints at something more. This occurs in the writings of Li the Elder (?635–?730), a mysterious figure loosely attached to Fazang's school of interpretation of the *Huayan Scripture*. Since the chronology of his writings is unclear, it is impossible to be sure that they are earlier than Fazang's work, though he was the older man, and indeed since he outlived Fazang his works seem to have been completed slightly later. Even so, there are strong indications that they were first drafted around the start of the century. Allegedly a distant relative of the ruling Li family, he appears to have been in touch with Fazang and indeed with court circles, but to have preferred to preserve his independence as a lay supporter, keeping to an eremitic existence in the area to the north where the Li family had originally been based. Li the Elder is interested in the way in which the worldview of the *Huayan Scripture* subverted commonsense notions of time and space, so the idea of a simultaneity that can embrace sequence is particularly appealing to him, and he uses the seal metaphor of Fazang yet more broadly to talk about such notions as 'root and branch', 'beginning and end', 'in between', 'duration' and 'length'. All these opposites, he says, in fact are bound up together, 'just as the precious seal of the ruler at a stroke imprints all, and completes a text without any "before" or "after"'.

This, then, is not a metaphor involving seals in general, but a specific seal, belonging to a ruler. So Li the Elder is not simply copying Fazang, but either drawing on a previously unmentioned detail in some earlier work that inspired both of them, or drawing on Fazang but modifying his metaphor independently. It looks like an allusion to something his contemporaries would have understood at once, but to what? Contemporary Buddhists in East Asia have now produced the means to search electronically all surviving Buddhist translations into Chinese, but no story about a ruler's seal and its qualities may be found in that entire corpus. This by no means eliminates the possibility that Li the Elder was referring to something in the Buddhist literature known to him and his readers, including Fazang. Apart from the translations that have come down to us, there were other texts available at this time in China which purported to be translations, but were often stories made up in the Indian fashion by Chinese Buddhists, and many of these were weeded out and not transmitted by later generations on the grounds that they were not authentic. Perhaps he was referring to something in one of these lost texts, which were widely accepted by most Buddhists other than the learned monks who compiled catalogues of what ought to be admitted to the Buddhist canon – and some works still in existence today actually got past them.

Even so, it is rare to find an allusion in Buddhist writing of the expository type produced by Li the Elder that cannot be located in the canonical corpus, and we must therefore ask ourselves if Li the Elder and his readers might perhaps have seen a ruler's precious seal in operation not in literature transmitted from the past, but in real life. Given the extent to which Chinese rulers tended to hold themselves aloof from the common people in well-protected environments like the Forbidden City that still exists in Beijing, what they did with their seals would have been more a matter of imagination than observation for all but a very few people. I have, however, introduced above the contribution to printing history made by the stamped security passes used in the imperial palace in the late seventh century, and it may be that these were so well known at the time that Li the Elder could refer to them without further explanation. But if so, then his terminology is not that used in the imperial bureaucracy itself. His use of words lies very much within the realm of Buddhist vocabulary exhibited in the canon, and in the *Huayan Scripture* itself. Some later figures, such as Zen masters, often made a point of referring to everyday objects and events in their exposition of Buddhist truth, but Li the Elder does not write in this way. So, then, could it be that he uses a term that does actually occur in passing in at least one translation of an Indian story (though not one in which the function of the seal is an issue), while expecting his readers to understand it as referring to something within their own environment? This something might, of course, be an object like a security pass. But in a sense it would be much more likely to refer to a woodblock-produced text, since if the *Great Spell* or anything else were distributed in this form, many more people would have become aware of the benefits of printing technology than would have noticed the production of imperial security passes.

None of this constitutes evidence that printing was used in China to disseminate the *Great Spell.* All that the writings of Fazang, Li the Elder and their contemporaries can show is that the basic advantages of printing technology would have been understood by the eminent religious persons of the day. But since the chances are that the knowledge that was required in order to deploy printing technology was already there in China before the late seventh century, in that the process of taking impressions of writing from engraved surfaces had by then probably come to be understood just as well as imposing patterns or writing from above by stamping, the main problem is to envisage circumstances in which, in a vibrant manuscript culture unparalleled in the medieval European experience, someone felt impelled to press home the advantages offered by printing despite the ready availability of manual copying. The preceding chapter left us with the hypothesis that an ambitious ruler in the Ashokan mould, having vowed to produce relics of the Buddha on such a scale that using words on paper in a vast number of multiple copies would have given the only likely chance of success, could well have encouraged experimentation with printing technology. But the foregoing account of Fazang and his activities in the first decade of the eighth century identifies reasons why, after the death of his ruler, this monk might have been spurred on to put earlier plans into effect. It would not have been any sentiments of loyalty to the departed, but guilt at betrayal, and fear of the possible spiritual consequences, that would have motivated him, and it would have been the need to do something quickly that would have impelled him to turn to printing to avert the danger.

Sadly, there seems to be no way at all to confirm this supposition. The disappearance of the copy of the *Great Spell* enshrined in 706 does not even allow us to be sure whether it was a printed copy or not, let alone who made it. I have come up with a scenario that at least fits all the known facts, but there is no clinching evidence to show that it was the only possible scenario. Some might even suspect that the invention of printing and its deployment by the state cannot have taken place in China at this time, or we would know more about it. For surely such a technology, even if it did not have the conspicuous impact that it had in Europe, would at least have had some detectable consequences. And what can be detected in China in the century or so following the dramatic events of 705? Little enough, perhaps, but, as the next chapter will show, not absolutely nothing. And, again, it is the activities of a woman that we must look to first.

CHAPTER EIGHT

FROM CONCUBINES TO CRIMINALS

In Europe the block printing of patterns and images on textiles forms an important part of the prehistory of printing, but when it comes to China I have so far made no reference to it.[1] This is not because it did not exist: block printing of textiles has taken place in China for well over two thousand years.[2] But it seems to have been confined at first to the luxury end of the market: typically metal blocks were used repeatedly in small areas with different colours to create intricate patterns on silk by stamping. It has been claimed that the printing of patterns on cheaper textiles goes back even further in ancient India, and it may be that an early Indian lead in this field made the stamping of Buddha images on paper a natural further step in Chinese Buddhist circles, though the proof for this is, yet again, missing.[3] But in the early eighth century in China it is possible to point to a technique that definitely did use wooden blocks too large to hold by hand rather than stamps in the dyeing of patterns on textiles. Even if this was still used only for luxury products, it provides evidence of technological progress that makes it highly probable that printing too had moved beyond hand-held stamps to the deployment of larger woodblocks to which the paper for printing was applied from above, rather than being laid out below a stamping instrument.

The best materials for studying this technology survive in Japan, where examples of complex polychrome images created on cloth by this means in the mid-eighth century have been preserved to this day, even if the earliest blocks still in existence are probably much later. The technique employed is quite clear, since it uses two tightly bound woodblocks as 'resists', that is, as devices to stop the natural spread of dyes through the cloth; other resists would include wax, or the 'tie and dye' approach, in which the cloth itself is tied so tightly in parts that the progress of the dye is halted. But in this Japanese technique the wooden blocks are intricately carved on both sides, so that while raised remains of the original surface are left on both blocks in mirror images of each other so as to form a pattern out of portions of the cloth from which the dye is excluded, other areas are carved out, to allow the dye to run freely. Typically, a piece of cloth squeezed in between the wooden blocks is folded over, so that a symmetrical image is obtained, as illustrations in books on Japanese art readily show.[4]

Now it is possible to calculate roughly when this innovation became known in China, since at least the family name of the woman responsible, which was Liu, is given in our source. This lady had an older sister and, because her family was rather a prominent one, the older sister was taken into the imperial harem of China's next great ruler, a grandson of the Chakravartin of the Golden Wheel who became the eventual beneficiary of the power struggles following her death, supplanting his own father in 712 and going on to reign for over four decades. In that year he appointed a new empress, and it is stated that the older sister served as her assistant. At some point, in order to mark her birthday, the younger sister gave a bolt of cloth that she had dyed using this technique she had invented herself not to her, but to her sister's superior, the empress. As a result, the benefits of her invention rapidly became known to

the emperor, who was so impressed that he ordered the manufac-
turing technique to be adopted as the exclusive privilege of his
imperial workshops, though soon enough (as the early Japanese
examples confirm) the secret became much more widely known.
Since the empress remained childless, and after beginning to lose her
husband's favour as early as 722 at the latest was dead (apparently of
natural causes) by 724, the probable date for Ms Liu's novel birthday
present for her sister's employer was some time in the second decade
of the eighth century. While it is possible that some unknown
artisan was responsible for developing the technique she used, and
that only its introduction to the palace should be credited to the
well-connected Ms Liu, creating textiles in traditional China was
very much seen as women's work, so it may well be – as our source
for this episode affirms, apparently on the basis of family tradition
recorded in the early ninth century – that young Ms Liu worked out
the entire technique herself.

In either case, what is intriguing about this technique is that it
uses not one but two woodblocks, carved in relief so as to fit
together. This is one stage more complex than carving blocks for
printing, so if Ms Liu was able to do this by *circa* 720, it makes it
much more probable that printers were already in operation before
that date using woodblocks rather than stamps. It is still, of course,
conceivable that the course of development was the other way
round, and that printing on paper took its cue from Ms Liu's invention. But the chances are that it was her observation of the art of
printing that gave her the idea of applying printing technology to
textiles by clamping two mirror-image carved wooden blocks
together over a piece of cloth. And at the very least, surviving examples of cloth dyed by this method provide very eloquent testimony
to what eighth-century East Asian woodworkers could do. This
ambiguity as to whether we are looking at a cause or a result of the
introduction of printing characterises the religious materials that
have been examined in the preceding chapter. There the tendency of

religious writers to talk about the automatic creation of writing by seals was simply taken as evidence that men like Fazang would have known what to do with printing if it were available to them, but one might equally well argue that it was their observation of woodblock printing that caused them all to start writing in this way, and that these metaphorical passages should be adduced as evidence for the impact of printing.

But just as all the evidence seems to be pointing towards some decisive shift in printing in China having taken place round about the year 700 or shortly thereafter, suddenly the picture changes and any further evidence becomes very hard to find. Worse than that, despite the new emperor's declared appreciation of textiles dyed using a woodblock technology, he seems to have gone out of his way to avoid using anything similar for the reproduction of texts. Like his grandfather, for example, he was a keen supporter of the family religion of Taoism, and especially later in his reign took a number of measures to support an even closer identification between the imperial line and its supposed divine ancestor, Laozi, the reputed author of the *Daode jing*. At one point, in 733, he even decreed that every household should possess a copy of this scripture, something that would imply, according to contemporary taxation statistics for his empire, the creation of no fewer than eight million manuscripts of this short text, though no doubt by this point in the dynasty quite a few copies had been made already, and indeed several dozen copies of Tang dynasty date survive to this day amongst the various versions to be found in the Dunhuang manuscripts.[5] But none of them are printed, and none of them even show traces of having been created in any special effort to supply a copy to every household. Where one does find that the state was involved in copying is in a version with the emperor's own commentary that was evidently for the use of civil service examination candidates. So while the bureaucracy provided for its own potential members, the populace was evidently expected to shift for itself; the most that was done to assist the general dissemination of the text was the provision of more copies inscribed on stone in various parts of the empire.[6] The model of dissemination here, then, is that used for centuries for the 'Confucian Classics', although the correct text of that much larger corpus was diffused from only a single point at the imperial capital whereas now a number of pillars bearing the *Daode jing* text were created in the provinces. Any thought of using 'automatic writing' other than rubbings taken from stone seems entirely absent, though whether through ignorance or a deliberate decision to stick to precedent and avoid novelty is not immediately clear.

If, however, one steps back and looks at the overall shift in the political and intellectual atmosphere that had taken place since the emperor's grandmother's day, their contrasting approaches to imperial ideology and to political practice emerge quite unambiguously.[7] Though in terms of religious history the shift is characterised by a switch from Buddhist justification of imperial rule back to the dynastic notion of rule by Taoist divine descent, this change of tack formed part of a much broader reorientation of government. His grandmother, the Great Sage Dowager Empress, whatever her private religious beliefs, had believed quite fervently in the twin values of promoting technology and an early form of 'globalisation'. This showed itself most conspicuously in her massive programmes of public works, in which non-Chinese were often involved. But such openness to novelty and to the outside world seems not to have been sustained, and this larger cultural shift shows itself in all sorts of ways. To cite just one example, the approach to his grandmother's tomb, unlike anything known in China before, features a very appealing carved ostrich, evidently taken from life. Later examples of carved ostriches may be found, but betray the fact that they are mere copies by artisans who had no idea what an ostrich really was.[8] The self-confident, cosmopolitan China of the seventh to early eighth centuries was already on the wane in the new emperor's time. Brilliant his court may have been, but there was already a mood of retrenchment abroad, even of hostility to foreigners, well before his reign was overwhelmed by rebellions sparked by one particular foreigner, a general ironically charged with keeping the 'barbarous' peoples of the northern frontier at bay. Could it be that a nascent printing industry fell prey to this larger cultural shift, and to its consequences in the field of religion?

Just two references from his reign hint at this possibility. One is an edict of 714 prohibiting laypersons from copying Buddhist texts, which were, according to the emperor's stipulations, to be left for monks only to recite.[9] Evidently a buoyant market for sutras had developed that threatened to overwhelm the production of Taoist texts, and though this may well have been a purely manuscript market, and there is nothing in the edict that suggests otherwise, it is just possible that the prospect of lay Buddhist publishers printing off sutras in such abundance and so cheaply as to give their religion a competitive edge prompted this imperial action. The effects of this edict are difficult to estimate, since it seems to have been copyists attached to monasteries who actually produced manuscript sutras for the lay believers whose names appear on them, and when printed sutras eventually appear, there is initially nothing to show that they were commercial products unconnected with monasteries either. By the time it is possible to find good evidence of printed sutras produced commercially, the dynasty had a purely nominal existence and was very close to its end.[10] The original motive for the imperial ban may have been sectarian, but the emperor was pragmatic enough not to be always implacably opposed to Buddhism, and even allowed his sister to promote the carving of the stone sutras mentioned in Chapter Three as designed to outlast the fading away of the Buddhist religion.[11] Some of his successors were even quite positive patrons of those forms of Buddhist belief that bolstered their position, even if they never returned to the full-scale Ashokan ideology espoused by the emperor's grandmother. If the ban on commercial sutra copying and printing was in place to the end of the dynasty, then perhaps other factors played a part.

It has been discovered, for example, that monasteries supported quite large numbers of copyists. A document from Dunhuang reveals that one temple there kept a staff of no fewer than fifty-five copyists, both monks and laymen.[12] Admittedly the institution concerned was quite a prominent one, and the dozen or so monasteries in Dunhuang may have carried greater administrative responsibilities than those in other parts of China. But even so the emperor's capital had well over one hundred monasteries in it, some of massive size, so that one may imagine several thousand copyists in that city alone who would no doubt have lobbied to keep the ban in place, especially since the Dunhuang document shows, by the repetition of the same family name, that copying sutras was probably for some a hereditary family business.[13] But if the printing entrepreneurs of eighth-century China were in fact kept out of their most lucrative market by a combination of imperial disfavour and longer-term vested interests, there is just one hint from the middle of the eighth century that they may have found other products by that date that made woodblock printing worthwhile. In 746 there is a record of another decree from the emperor declaring that the penalty for forging a freehand 'seal' (an identifying mark that today would be called a signature) was to be the same as for forging a cast or engraved seal.[14] Why had the use of freehand seals become so widespread that this measure was necessary? Could it be that too many seal-carvers had been lured away to another, new industry? Might some of the undated spells that archaeologists have recovered – which are always and quite possibly deliberately printed in formats that distinguish them from the 'proper' full sutras produced by professional copyists – represent products of that new industry? Nothing in our sources so far confirms this, but even for the late eighth century it is possible to learn a little more about woodblocks, and what information there is tends to confirm at least one of the other factors that may have influenced China's rulers against resorting to the new technology.

In Chapter Two it was noted that the carving of inscriptions on stone was deemed a worthy activity for emperors, in that the First Emperor of China had himself marked his new territory by a series of inscriptions on China's mountains. One of these inscriptions had evidently become so popular with later admirers of its calligraphy that the villagers at the foot of the mountain were always being sent up on expeditions by officials who wanted to make rubbings, to the extent that they decided to break up the inscription into pieces by burning it. Unfortunately this did nothing to stop orders to go and make rubbings from the remains, so in the end a substitute inscription was made. But accounts of it vary: in the late eighth century it is described as having been made of wood; in the early ninth it is asserted that a local official was responsible for making a replica of stone to stand in the county offices for any interested party to take a rubbing.[15] One possible conclusion from this is to suppose that locally the inscription was first re-created in wood, and then when the locality could afford it or its magistrate felt compassionate enough to provide, the stone substitute was erected instead. This possibility is certainly increased by what we learn of the re-creation under the Tang dynasty of the 'stone classics', the massive inscription bearing the text of the entire corpus of Confucian writing that was also mentioned in the second chapter. By this time damage and loss had made the creation of a new version imperative, but the revision and editing of such a large corpus was too large an undertaking for anything to be done in a hurry. In 776, however, a provisional text was established at the capital and carved on wooden panels, while scholarly debate continued. It was only in 837, by which time the wooden panels were beginning to weather, that the dynasty finally succeeded in erecting a complete set of inscriptions in stone.[16] Again, the function of these inscriptions was to provide standard texts that could be copied by rubbing in a way guaranteed to eliminate the errors of freehand manuscript transmission. But although both wood and stone were equal in this regard, the long-term and constant use envisaged for the 'Confucian classics' as generation after generation made use of them meant that stone was the preferred solution, and wood a temporary expedient. The same would have applied to the First Emperor's inscription, and it was perhaps the deterioration of their wooden substitute that made the weary inhabitants of the neighbourhood relieved when their magistrate provided something more permanent.

Where there would appear to be a record of the use of wood in the creation of a text of much more ephemeral interest in 798, without any reference to a place where the inscribed wood was to be found, the chances are that we really are dealing with a woodblock for printing, not just a temporary expedient to take the place of stone as a source for rubbings, though for reasons to be considered shortly that cannot be entirely ruled out. But the creation of this text has been generally overlooked so far, because it has been overshadowed by its owner's involvement in one of the best-documented cases of the officially sanctioned copying of a large quantity of manuscripts.[17] The evidence on both enterprises has, moreover, been preserved not in China but in Japan. Already in dealing with Fazang's Korean contacts in the preceding chapter I have remarked on the transmission of books via diplomatic contacts, and in the case of the somewhat more sporadic contacts between China and Japan (the journey to China was much more daunting than for Koreans at the time) obtaining Chinese books to boost the stock of knowledge available in a country still emerging from a largely oral culture was one of the primary objectives of the whole exercise.[18] The owner of the neglected document was, however, not a diplomat but a monk, since Buddhist knowledge was accounted just as important as secular knowledge, if not more so, and indeed he proved so successful in acquiring new Buddhist texts and importing new forms of Buddhism that from the late ninth century he has been known in Japan as 'The Great Master who Transmitted the Teachings'. In 803, however, when he went to China, the future Great Master was a comparative nonentity, and because he decided (or was obliged) to study at the great Buddhist centres near where his ship arrived in present-day Zhejiang rather than travel to the capital, he risked losing out in career terms to others who did make the full journey to the centre of the contemporary East Asian world order. But during less than nine months of foreign study he gained the support of the local Chinese authorities in making copies of a large number of Buddhist texts. Specifically, twenty copyists, using 8,532 sheets of paper, created 120 new manuscripts in less than two months.

The rate of copying – which was doubtless only the fastest that could guarantee a very high level of accuracy – is not that impressive when measured against the rates achieved by contemporary Western European monks, since it implies a daily production that could have been in single figures, while a Carolingian scribe was capable of eleven pages a day; certainly Japanese copyists of the period worked at about seven pages a day. But looked at from another angle the final results of his stay (which included other purchases) saw the Great Master produce an eventual catalogue of 222 newly imported works after his return to Japan in 805, and although this was rather a small manuscript collection by contemporary Chinese standards, a contemporary Carolingian librarian seems to have counted himself lucky to accession sixty-seven new manuscripts in more than thirty years.[19] Another notable difference may be found in the additional material associated with several of the catalogues brought back by the Great Master, which includes his correspondence with the Chinese local authorities giving him letters under their seals authorising the entire enterprise. One reason for this may have been that the Chinese state was always nervous about exporting books in case the knowledge they contained might be used against it, and the Great Master, separated from the main body of his embassy, was particularly vulnerable to bureaucratic harassment.[20] But if restrictions on copying Buddhist texts were still in place, then perhaps the need to possess documentation to show that all his manuscripts had been acquired in a legitimate fashion was also in his mind. At least one of his later followers, aware of this precedent, seems to have taken very similar precautions.[21]

The Great Master, however, was clearly a realist, and perhaps reckoned that even if he left China with his bibliographical trophies intact, someone might make trouble for him in Japan. He was, after all, bringing back newfangled ideas that the existing Buddhist establishment was not necessarily too keen on, yet he was not the only monk in Japan trying to build a career on his success in studying abroad. In 821 we find him compiling a dossier concerning his studies in China in order to emphasise their value, and it is in this dossier that there has been transmitted a short document, not mentioned in his earlier catalogue, in praise of his Chinese teacher by a Chinese official – a very lowly official from the bottom rung of the bureaucratic hierarchy, but an official even so.[22] It is this piece, dated to 798, which its author describes as having been carved into wood. How did the Great Master acquire it? He already had a manuscript biography of his Chinese teacher, which he had prevailed upon a Chinese fellow student to provide, and this is listed (though under a slightly misleading title) in his catalogue. Did this sheet of paper arrive in Japan via some other traveller, to be incorporated into his dossier just to bulk out its contents and help stress the importance of the Great Master's study in China? Or had he already obtained it on his trip 'on the side', as it were, and kept it apart from his official, authenticated acquisitions as a cheap and purely personal souvenir of his adventures? Since the piece may well have been purchased in a Buddhist monastery, there is nothing to suggest that it was the product of illegal printing – its author seems not to be expecting any adverse outcome for his bureaucratic career as the result of his work – but his exact motive is unclear. Perhaps he just felt that it would help his image to be seen as the patron of a highly regarded monk who had himself studied with a yet more famous master.

This piece may still represent no more than a record of an inscription in wood made by someone not quite wealthy enough to create an inscription in stone – though a stone inscription for a living person would have been somewhat unusual, for the Kafkaesque reason that most people did not like to commit to such a durable medium positive opinions about anyone who might yet blot their copybook and involve them in guilt by association. But if I am right in seeing it as deriving from a printed object, then it does give us a clue to the type of single-sheet product that was already being produced in provincial centres far away from the great and good of the metropolitan elite that dominates our sources. It is, however, one of this group, sent out to end his career as an important provincial governor, who provides our next reference to the printed word, on 24 December 835, not long before the Chinese New Year of 22 January.[23] He asks the emperor to ban the printing of calendars, because in the areas of present-day Sichuan and the north side of the lower Yangzi valley he has noticed that even before the government has distributed the official calendar, private printers are flooding the market with their own products, undermining the proprieties of 'respectful provision' – an allusion to the legendary first sage ruler of China, whose respectful provision of a calendar embodied his caring attitude towards his subjects. That his complaint was not without foundation is demonstrated by the survival of a small fragment of a printed calendar from the preceding year, 834, which constitutes the oldest piece of dated printing material from China.[24] Control of information on the passing year, so essential in an agrarian society, had been a key aspect of legitimate rule since times long past. But the calendar, with additional information on lucky and unlucky days was – and still is – a numinous object in itself, a prize possession even for barely literate households. One can see why the seasonal demand for such a work could have made resort to printing a very reasonable proposition, and if this ban had been enforceable, the progress of the new technology would certainly have been further hampered. But the authority of the dynasty, which had been patchy since a great rebellion in the middle of the eighth century, became during the course of the ninth century progressively less effective in local society, even where nominally under government jurisdiction.

Under such circumstances, moreover, printing was not the only means of making money out of selling pieces of paper. Already in 824 one local warlord was conducting an excellent trade in selling the ordination certificates required of monks by the government, which granted immunity from taxation. According to the estimate of an outraged loyalist official – an able administrator not given to wild exaggeration – he was already within sight of shifting no fewer than 600,000 copies.[25] One might naturally suspect that such a staggering figure could only be reached by means of printing, but the first account of the printing of such documents relates to the eleventh century, and the only earlier surviving examples (though these admittedly amount to no more than two provisional certificates found among the Dunhuang manuscripts) are stamped with official seals but otherwise handwritten.[26] The monastery whence the warlord conducted his trade was an unusually large one that exploited its advantageous position on a major transport route to attract large numbers of pilgrims, so it could well have had the clerical means to generate such a large number of manuscript items anyhow.[27]

Even well-born members of the governing elite had not been averse to a little peculation at the best of times, so upstart warlords probably felt few inhibitions in emulating them. High officials a long way from home tended to take ample measures beyond their generous salaries to compensate themselves for having to serve so far from the delights of metropolitan culture, and no governorship was better known for the opportunities it afforded for corruption than that based in present-day Canton. In July 855 one occupant of this lucrative posting had just been caught with his hand in the till and reassigned to a sinecure in the erstwhile Holy Capital, which had by now suffered a long eclipse to become a sort of bureaucratic ghost town, still culturally important but governed only by those whose careers had been deliberately sidetracked, while all the political action was centred on the court at Chang'an, present-day Xi'an. But these two centres were not that far apart, and our ex-governor seems to have hit upon a cunning ruse to redeem himself. Presumably financing himself with the remains of his ill-gotten gains, he printed off 'several thousand' copies of a short work on how to counteract alchemical poisoning. During this period both the ruling house and its higher civil servants were caught up in a vogue for seeking immortality through ingesting alchemical preparations that all too often caused madness and premature death, so his little tract would have found a ready readership. It is known that his work did reach the court, and a recently published inscription shows that he eventually died with his high rank and titles restored to him, so his venture in politically motivated charitable publishing must be accounted a success.[28]

But this would seem to be the very first instance of any member of the Tang elite sponsoring any publication by printing, and the circumstances turn out to be far from ordinary. One potentially useful piece of information that remains unknown is the dates of our eminent crook's birth and death, but it seems that he was well on towards the end of his career when he took to printing, so it may be that again time was a factor in his calculations, and this effort at rehabilitating himself was the act of an old man in a hurry. This is the last case of printing that I have so far been able to investigate in detail. In the second half of the ninth century references to printing, plus a few scraps of printed materials with dates on, begin to become slightly more plentiful, so rather than squeeze as much information as possible out of single references, it becomes possible to talk about patterns of printing activity.[29] These at the very least do nothing to dispel the suspicion that the development of printing was subject to restraints that are not always discernible to us today, even if important factors such as the extraordinarily high standards of productivity achieved by Chinese manuscript culture are plain enough.

A couple of sources preserve accounts of what printed materials were for sale in book markets in the late ninth century. Calendars and almanacs are mentioned, as are works on divination and other reference materials such as dictionaries, medical works and clan rules. Buddhist sutras are not mentioned in this context, though there is one record of the monastic printing of materials concerned with Buddhist canon law. References in Japanese monkish catalogues, transcriptions into manuscript of printers' colophons, and surviving printed materials confirm this range of publications, and some of the materials concerned have been subject to specialist studies published in English.[30] But nothing published by the state is there, nor is anything published by anyone from the upper echelons of society, and nor yet is there any Buddhist material clearly of commercial origins other than spells written out in formats quite unlike those of a normal sutra. In the tenth century or slightly before, with the waning and eventual ending of the dynasty, the pattern changes, not simply with the advent of the commercial publishing of sutras, but with the rise of state printing and the emergence of printed poetry and prose of the type favoured by the educated elite. These changes deserve careful scrutiny in future. In some cases they were far from instantaneous – it is possible to point, for example, to one high minister of the mid-century who printed his own writings and ended up being laughed at for his vulgarity, suggesting that printing was still not fully accepted in some circles.[31] But for the first two centuries or so of printing it is time now to state a few conclusions, even if they must remain somewhat tentative, pending further research.

CHAPTER NINE

FILLING IN THE BLANKS

Although the preceding chapters have added a number of new sources to the discussion of the origins of printing, my account of all the possible evidence for printing itself has been by no means exhaustive, especially as compared with some recent studies in Chinese.[1] Instead, much more has been said about the religious background, because it is my belief that without a good understanding of the religious ideas of the age the emergence of printing in China simply does not make sense. Even in this area no attempt has been made to cover every possible angle. I have noted, for example, that the accuracy provided by printing as a means of copying a text was well understood by the late seventh century. But this may have had religious significance in some circumstances where texts were used with an eye to their scrutiny by beings in the spirit world, since the gods were believed to disapprove of sloppy copying.[2] At times, therefore, well-to-do believers of this period would go to extraordinary lengths to make sure that scriptures written on their behalf were produced as accurately as possible in conditions of ritual purity.[3] Eliminating human beings from the process perhaps achieved the same goal, though it should be recognised that it was the government's search for a means to disseminate accurate texts that resulted in the tenth-century printing of the 'Confucian' canon, and then the entire Buddhist canon, with the Taoist canon also printed eventually in a government-sponsored edition.

It is these major government enterprises that emerge most clearly in our sources, for in China the greater part of historical writing was produced by bureaucrats for bureaucrats.[4] Religious works therefore have a particular value in allowing us to escape from this bias. But one hypothesis put forward in the last chapter about the dominance of copyists in Buddhist monasteries should make us beware another possible bias in the very materials that would at first sight seem to offer the best evidence for social conditions at this time. For the Dunhuang manuscripts – our only substantial source for surviving contemporary documents unaltered by later editors – derive from a Buddhist monastic library, and not a very well financed monastery library at that.[5] If only a couple of dozen or so printed items may be found amongst these manuscripts is this really testimony to printing's irrelevance even right up to the start of the eleventh century, when this archive was closed?[6] Or did the impact of printing lie elsewhere, in ordinary homes, about which we know virtually nothing?

So questions still abound, and some further reflection on issues of possible bias would also seem to be in order. But first, let us look at the way in which an understanding of the religious background can help us to explain some features of the rise of printing in China that make it quite spectacularly unlike the spread of printing in Europe. The earliest printed materials, after all, were designed to be distributed but not read, and show up not in China, where all the development towards printing appears to have been taking place, but as far away as Japan. In China itself, by contrast, the cluster of interesting references in our sources round about CE 700 seems to give way to a prolonged period of ostensible inactivity, until in the ninth century printing starts to appear at the margins of the picture. Meanwhile, we should note, in Korea and Japan at this time the picture is a complete blank. Add in religion, however, and especially religion in relation to the state, and a number of fragmentary pieces of the jigsaw fall into place.

Let us summarise what we have been able to discover. The technological requirements for the invention of woodblock printing were in all probability already in place in the late fifth century CE, but in a manuscript culture that already possessed abundant supplies of paper and also the writing brush, an instrument that made rapid copying of texts relatively easy. Multiple copies therefore were easily created by hand, and it was not until after the following century, a time of great social and religious turmoil, that the need arose for the creation of short texts on a massive scale, beyond the scope of the existing technology. These short texts were not designed to be read, but to serve as words of the Buddha construed as relics embodying his continued presence in this world, since the events of the sixth century had highlighted the doctrine that the Buddha's influence, destined eventually to wither away to nothing, was already on the wane. This notion of Buddha's words as relics was of particular importance to China's rulers, who needed to calm the fears of their subjects by demonstrating that they could distribute relics in large numbers across their domains. An empress of the Tang dynasty who, uniquely in Chinese history, succeeded to her husband's position to rule in her own right, and even under her own dynastic title in 690 was, according to our sources, especially interested in ways of creating large numbers of relics. Towards the end of her life in 705 she would also have been interested in multiplying copies of a 'great spell', a newly translated Buddhist text promising its propagator extraordinary benefits in this life and in that to come. Since it is this very work that turns up by the mid-eighth century in printed form in Korea and was printed in a million copies by another empress slightly later in Japan, the presumption must be that the text was actually distributed across East Asia in quantity by printing either in 705 or more likely as part of funerary rituals for the former empress in 706. But the restoration of the Tang dynasty brought about the revival of Taoist methods of legitimising imperial rule based on assertions of divine descent, and the empress and all her works became an unpleasant memory, mentioned as little as possible. Commercial booksellers, who might have used the technique to produce popular Buddhist texts in quantity, were forbidden to deal in Buddhist literature, which became the exclusive province of the large population of professional copyists attached to Buddhist institutions. China's educated elite, too, found no need to move beyond the use of manuscript.

But commercial publishers did come to employ printing for the production of short spells reformatted to distinguish them from integral Buddhist texts, and for calendars, where speedy high-volume production was of the essence. By the end of the eighth century, perhaps, and certainly by the middle of the ninth, one or two other individuals also found printing worthwhile in some circumstances. As the powers of the dynasty declined, commercial printers extended their range to include a number of reference works, while Buddhist establishments also began to employ the technology. By about 900 the commercial printing of Buddhist texts appears, and in the following century, after the formal extinction of the dynasty in 907, state printing as well. Once employed by the state, woodblock printing became both widely known and accepted at all levels of society. By the twelfth century printing using movable wooden type was common in north-west China, and possibly other parts, where it continued to be used in later times. During the existence of the Mongol empire it would seem that woodblock printing and in all probability movable wooden type became known in Europe, though, as discussed in Chapter One, the latter would have been impossible for Europeans to emulate, with the result that movable type had to wait until the inventions of Gutenberg and others in the fifteenth century.

Earlier accounts, to be fair, have emphasised the Buddhist penchant for multiplying texts, though only recently has it been realised that for some Mahayana pioneers exhortations to copy texts helped propagate what was originally a minority movement. And, despite some awareness of the importance of Ashoka to Chinese Buddhism and to printing, without the clue provided by the message from Songshan no one was able to identify the dual role of the *Great Spell* in allowing East Asian rulers both to emulate Ashoka and to pursue personal goals. Both roles could be brought together and described as a 'ritual' use of printing, since the printed material was not designed for reading. Without further explanation, however, this term runs the risk of creating misunderstanding, allowing those who wish to dismiss Chinese printing as irrelevant to characterise it as having been put to no practical purpose, as the invention of gunpowder is dismissed as merely leading to the invention of fireworks. We may today consider the old empress misguided in her hopes of the personal material benefits that might derive from the multiplication of the *Great Spell* – though the practice of religion for the material benefits it may bring is with us yet in both East and West – but in that its printing could have aided her in playing the part of Chakravartin of the Golden Wheel, the potential political benefits were entirely practical: 'ritual' as to their context, but no less effective in asserting her right to rule. Her hopes and fears were in some respects very much of her age, and may perhaps have been more intelligible to Bede than they now are to us. But her political skills in legitimising her rule would surely win the appreciation of any politician today, and the political use of religion is just as much part of our world as of hers.

Of course different historians will always see things differently, depending on the nature of their interests. The late Denis Twitchett, who composed what is still the best short survey of printing in China as long ago as 1977, was a historian of institutions with a keen eye to legal and other social aspects of printing, though he was also well aware of religious elements, such as the example of Ashoka. The very last comment on my own explorations of printing I received from him concerned the disgraced governor of Canton's financing of the distribution in print of a remedy for alchemical poisoning. To him this raised all sorts of issues as to how texts of any sort were distributed. But if information on this vital topic survives, I have not noticed it, and possibly never will. Only someone with an excellent knowledge of the vocabulary of Tang bureaucratic procedure is likely to spot the key sentence that reveals how things were done, if it exists. To be honest, even the new suggestions I have made on the basis of my knowledge of religious history are only the outcome of a somewhat unusual situation in China, so that the task of adding in information on religious history to the picture has fallen to me by default. For the first three decades of the existence of the People's Republic of China the study of religious beliefs in history remained an underdeveloped area, and even today it is not usually combined with the study of technology. Religion was, and to some extent still is, seen as part of the superstitious, 'feudal' past, holding China back, while technology – paper, printing, gunpowder and the compass – is seen as one of the glories of Chinese civilisation, pointing the way to a more scientific future. Research into the beneficial aspects of the Taoist tradition, clearly a Chinese product, has been in any case more enthusiastically pursued than research into the contribution of Buddhism, an alien faith, to the betterment of Chinese society.

This bias in research is not necessarily the result of Chinese nationalism, since much the same reluctance to deal with Buddhism may be found in the early writings of Joseph Needham. Indeed, as late as 1978 a republication of his thoughts on the matter still states baldly that some Buddhist beliefs 'tragically played a part in strangling the growth of Chinese science', though in the one substantial conversation I had with him, a few years later, he readily conceded that at the start of his investigations he had been unduly critical of Buddhism.[7] It was the notion of the world as illusion in Mahayana

Buddhism that troubled him most, though that idea has a religious rather than scientific function, and some Buddhists at least distinguished the level of illusion from the workings of the world in which we live: if one sees a rope and thinks it is a snake, the illusion causes our pulse to quicken anyhow. There is however another element in Needham's writing that does seem to fit more readily with the narrative of the birth of printing summarised above. He had a tendency – not entirely justified in the light of more recent research – to think well of Taoism, because he saw it as playing a part that could not be found elsewhere in Chinese civilisation.[8] The mainstream school of thinking of the bureaucratic Chinese elite, or 'Confucianism' (another problematic term) in his vocabulary, seemed to him to be less interested in science and technology, and to have 'turned its face away from Nature'.[9] Ironically, the dynasty that apparently turned away from printing from 706 till its demise in 907 was as Taoist as any in Chinese history, though perhaps its 'state Taoism' would have seemed a corrupt and inauthentic business to Needham. Even so, it published no general regulations against printing, so although China was in theory at least as tightly controlled then as now, it is not possible to invoke some stereotypical 'oriental despotism' as an inhibiting factor. Rather one must surely look, as Needham did, to the culture of the broader elite for some explanation of their general reluctance to make more than occasional use of what seems to us an obvious technological advance.

There is certainly a strain in Tang writing that evinces a strong horror of vulgarity, and indeed this may even take the form – more or less – of saying that no one worth their salt will be at all intelligible to the common herd.[10] That is presumably why printing one's own work was still found quite risible in the mid-tenth century, and even much later writers will frequently aver that they would never have thought of publishing their works had their friends not prevailed upon them to do so. Printing just looked far too commercial to the dedicated gentleman and amateur, who would copy out the poetry he really liked rather than buy it by the book-load. Poets who did become more widely popular even seem to have found success worrying, in that they could not guarantee the authenticity of the works transmitted beyond their own circle of friends, and indeed sometimes found works incorrectly attributed to them. To issue a printed edition, however, would entail the presumption of continued popularity, which was hardly good for one's image. True hermits, of course, allegedly wrote their compositions on rocks and trees, not caring about their ultimate fate. Even for less socially detached persons, the deliberate courting of an audience usually went no further in Tang times than leaving a poem inscribed on an inn wall.[11] There was, in short, an undeniable snobbery about authorship which is not entirely absent in Renaissance Europe, but which there was more vulnerable to market forces. The Tang, by contrast, was a self-consciously aristocratic dynasty to the end, and only its passing allowed new rulers and a new, broader ruling class to come to the fore.

And perhaps even more of a constraint came from force of habit: every fast track career in the Tang civil service began in the imperial library, copying books. Only when this skill had been demonstrated did an appointment to any administrative post follow.[12] No doubt this training inculcated the sense that multiple copies were the prerogative of the emperor, just as growing up as a copyist in a Buddhist monastery (or, *mutatis mutandis,* in a Taoist temple) no doubt inculcated the belief that only canonical religious literature, which was subject to government scrutiny for conformity to the officially sanctioned canon, might form an exception. Even without explicit anti-printing regulations, one might have felt slightly nervous about going beyond conventional limits, since the state was certainly authoritarian, and jealous of its prerogatives. But equally, the combination of ink, brush and paper constituted a technology of information so efficient that no search for alternatives seemed particularly pressing. There was more of a need in those parts of the

East Asian world that lacked a well-established scribal culture, though there – I am thinking primarily of Japan – there was not a ready market for books either, for many centuries. Of course, where text was used to reach large numbers of people, the results were impressive. The great popular religious reformer Ippen (1239–89) tells us quite precisely, for example, that he distributed no fewer than 251,724 copies of the printed invocation of Amida that lay at the heart of his own Japanese religious movement.[13] This printed propagation of religion certainly had an impact, but does it 'count' in the history of printing? If so, then the entire early history of printing laid out in the preceding chapters might serve as a warning that one does not have to print 'books' as normally understood to achieve an impact on society, and that by looking for printed books amongst the educated elite and religious clergy of Tang times as evidence for the impact of printing we may be deceiving ourselves.[14] If we take the European case described by Eisenstein and others as the norm, then perhaps not finding the same phenomenon in China is simply blinding us to the existence of something much more interesting there from about 700 to 1000 that deserves investigation in its own right, as a tale not of absence or failure, but of a society where the fully literate had all the books they needed, but print allowed the less educated greater access to some elements of print culture for the first time, and this in turn brought about palpable but subtle changes not immediately visible in sources deriving from the fully literate minority.

But Needham's suspicions about negative factors can be viewed from a slightly different perspective, one that perhaps did not occur to a man of his generation. For even in 1960 one Chinese account of the period covered in the preceding narrative lays the troubles of the dynasty quite unselfconsciously at the door of women and foreigners.[15] Such was the traditional perception of the Chinese historian, and of the Chinese males who dominate our sources. If judged in terms of today's terminology, they would certainly all be found guilty of racism and sexism. When, for example, the contemporary reader consults one major compilation of materials concerning the Tang put together in 1814, a quick survey of its contents shows that it devotes more than nine-tenths of its vast bulk to writings produced by royalty and by educated males, after which right at the end comes an assortment of lesser categories of author in descending order of importance: Buddhist and Taoist clergy, women, unidentified and anonymous, eunuchs and, last of all, foreigners. Yet looking back at the narrative of progress that can still be retrieved from Chinese sources, one notes that technological change was promoted by the eunuch Cai Lun with his improvements to paper manufacture, and by Ms Liu, the concubine's sister and innovator in dyeing techniques. And if the scene I have imagined as being witnessed by the Venerable Bede bears any relation to the truth, then a woman and a half-foreign Buddhist clergyman played a decisive role in the introduction of printing also. New technologies reached the centre of power through the court's contacts beyond the bureaucracy. But the bureaucrats wrote the history, so credit tended not to be given to those to whom it was due. Scholars only know of Ms Liu, for example, as a result of family tradition committed to writing much later.

So the part played by the woman who discovered printing in adapting Chinese technology to Indian religious goals is ultimately something that can only be guessed at. As Tang dynastic control reasserted itself after its temporary displacement by the Zhou dynasty – an episode of political discontinuity even today glossed over in almost all books on Chinese history published anywhere, which list the Tang as uninterrupted – a great deal of rewriting of history went on, the details of which are by no means easy to unravel. The earliest official history that survives goes back to the mid-tenth century, after the dynasty ended, but for information on the period of greatest relevance to her activities it depends largely on materials first compiled in the middle of the eighth century itself.[16] In the few newly added tenth-century portions of the text as it now exists there is an unmistakable and overt hostility towards her, her titles being stripped away to a minimal equivalent of 'Ms Wu' in the first stage of a post-dynastic process of rewriting that was to culminate in the next century in a thoroughgoing attempt at eliminating systematically any reference to her ever having ruled as emperor at all. This posthumous coup, carried out bloodlessly but with great ruthlessness by later historians, was followed by further centuries of more or less constant denigration, with very few dissenting voices. But during the first phase of writing up her reign in the eighth century official historians could not be so harsh: to vilify the grandmother of the ruling emperor without running the risk of sullying his reputation as well was a task probably beyond even the most subtle of them, so the basic policy seems to have been to say the barest minimum about her reign.

Least said, soonest mended, then, and in this case recourse to religious materials – despite the one or two fragments of evidence discussed above – does not help us much, since after the Tang restoration the Buddhist establishment was profoundly embarrassed by its conspicuous support for the usurpation and its subsequent flagrant enjoyment of the trappings of power, and so tended to stick by the same maxim, as did Taoists equally embarrassed by their less than perfect loyalty to the divinely descended Li family. If anything, now Buddhists were especially anxious to assert that their religion was not to do with outward display, but an inward thing – a turn of events that was of some consequence for the rise of Zen Buddhism.[17] Even so, the indications would seem to be that though Chinese today may rightly take pride in the inventions of printing, paper, gunpowder and the compass, in the case of printing it was an untypical China that was able to draw upon the talents of women and foreigners to a far greater extent than usually was the case. And for that mankind has to thank one very untypical woman, one so able that she not only deployed her talents to achieve the highest position open to her in her society but also went on quite uniquely to win the highest position of all, the emperorship. In the short term her achievements were, it seems, deliberately ignored. Her very epitaph remained unwritten. But surely as China once more opens up to the world, and seeks to draw on the talents of all its citizens, her achievements should not be forgotten anywhere in the world where printed books are read.

This is not to deny the importance of Johannes Gutenberg. He may not have been responsible for all the innovations that allowed printing to get under way in Europe, but he certainly played a major part, and his contribution should not be contested, as it once was. At the same time it is necessary to observe that even in Elizabeth Eisenstein's account of her 'revolution' she gives full credit to the part played by woodblock in the early printing of illustrations.[18] And the story of woodblock has to be a much longer one, with a full cast of characters: not just one heroic inventor figure, but a range of discoverers and disseminators who gradually adapted and improved some basic techniques to new situations. That story stretches back through the nameless slaves who brought their techniques to Europe, back to the corrupt ex-governor of Canton, and even further, to the unreliable pilgrim Yijing and his accounts of India, right back to the would-be magus Gong Xuanxuan and his wonderful block of jade. One would hardly typify most of them as heroic, and if heroism must be unsullied by the moral taint of murder (albeit mostly in self-defence), especially not the woman whose part in the discovery of printing I have considered the most crucial. But perhaps it is our own romantic obsession with genius that prevents us from seeing the more sordid truth about human progress.

Or is that too negative a verdict? In writing this book I have been very conscious of using my own earlier research to an uncomfortable extent – easy, because I am familiar with it, but worrisome in that I am particularly familiar with its fallibility. No one researching the beginnings of printing in Europe is put in that situation. How reliable are the assertions made in the preceding pages? Common sense suggests that they cannot be as solid as findings that have been scrutinised by hundreds of scholars over decades. But where are the scholars to do that?[19] If Chinese history impinges at all on the consciousness of most students of Chinese at the moment, it is merely as background. The thought that a study of Chinese history might actually raise problems of any interest is – to judge by the complete absence of posts in British history departments fully devoted to pre-modern China – not one that is widely shared. My own opinion, however, is that the study of the religious elements in the rise of Chinese printing entails not only a confrontation with all sorts of stimulating questions, but also an encounter with the lives of other human beings in other times and places, some of whom at least emerge from the record with a vividness that does not fail to impress, despite the vast distance that separates their experience from ours. I would like to think that one day historians of the future might perhaps be a little puzzled by our failure to do more to make the connection.

NOTES

Chapter One: The View from Jarrow

1. This information from the nomad embassy is now translated in Michael and Mary Whitby, *The History of Theophylact Simocatta* (Oxford: Clarendon Press, 1986), pp. 191–2.
2. For one recent fictional account of her life in English, see Shan Sa, *Empress: A Novel* (New York: Regan Books, 2006). Other recent popular treatments are Jonathan Clements, *Wu: The Chinese Empress Who Schemed, Seduced and Murdered Her Way to Become a Living God* (Stroud, Gloucestershire: Sutton Publishing, 2007) and Nigel Cawthorne, *Daughter of Heaven: The True Story of the Only Woman to Become Emperor of China* (Oxford: Oneworld, 2007).
3. Antonino Forte, 'The Maitreyist Huaiyi (D. 695) and Taoism', *Tang yanjiu* 4 (1998), pp. 15–29.
4. Charles D. Benn, *The Cavern-Mystery Transmission: A Taoist Ordination Rite of AD 711* (Honolulu: University of Hawaii Press, 1991), pp. 5–6.
5. Even if later legend would have preferred to think otherwise: see Volker Klöpsch, 'Lo Pin-wang's Survival: Traces of a Legend', *T'ang Studies* 6 (1988), pp. 77–97.
6. An excellent modern print, made using traditional methods, by the contemporary artist Yang Feng, depicting Chinese printing almost twelve centuries before the artist's birth may be found in Anne Farrer, ed., *Chinese Printmaking Today: Woodblock Printing in China 1980–2000* (London: British Library, 2003), p. 120. The introductory essay in this volume by David Barker, 'Woodblock Printing in China: Tools and Techniques', pp. 36–42, is an important and readable account of the continuity between traditional and modern methods.

7. Note John M. Hobson, *The Eastern Origins of Western Civilisation* (Cambridge: Cambridge University Press, 2004), pp. 22–3, on the too ready dismissal of non-European developments in a volume that makes a lively – indeed polemical – argument for changing our outlook.

8. The discussion that follows in this chapter is based primarily on T. H. Barrett, 'Comparison and the Art of the Book: Some Stereotypes Explored', in Ming Wilson and Stacey Pierson, eds, *The Art of the Book in China* (London: The Percival David Foundation, 2006), pp. 251–63.

9. S. H. Steinberg, *Five Hundred Years of Printing* (Harmondsworth: Penguin, 1961), p. 156.

10. John Man, *The Gutenberg Revolution: The Story of a Genius and an Invention that Changed the World* (London: Review, 2002), p. 90.

11. See Tim Brook, *The Chinese State in Ming Society* (Abingdon: RoutledgeCurzon, 2005), pp. 118–36, and especially pp. 127–8; Haun Saussy, *Great Walls of Discourse and Other Adventures in Cultural China* (Cambridge, Mass.: Harvard University Press, 2001), pp. 17–19.

12. John Barrow, *Travels in China* (1806), as quoted by David Martin Jones, *The Image of China in Western Social and Political Thought* (Basingstoke: Palgrave, 2001), p. 41.

13. This has already been touched on in T. H. Barrett, 'Ignorance and the Technology of Information: Some Comments on China's Knowledge of the West on the Eve of the "Western Invasion"', *Asian Affairs* XXVI (old series vol. 82), Part 1 (February 1995), pp. 20–32. The 'rare periodical', the *Canton Miscellany* of 1831, is described in n. 32 of this study.

14. Christopher A. Reed, *Gutenberg in Shanghai: Chinese Print Capitalism, 1876–1937* (Vancouver: UBC Press, 2004), pp. 42–3; cf. Hubert W. Spillett, 'A Catalogue of Scriptures in the Languages of China and the Republic of China' (London: British and Foreign Bible Society, 1975), p. 7.

15. For lithography, see Reed, *Gutenberg in Shanghai*, pp. 97–104, who notes that Chinese printers were soon using the new technology to outpace missionary presses using letterpress. For the persistence of woodblock also in missionary circles, see Spillett 'Catalogue of Scriptures', p. 49, concerning a publication of 1889.

16. Compare Sterling Seagrave, *The Soong Dynasty* (London: Sidgwick & Jackson, 1986), p. 59, and Kai-wing Chow, *Publishing, Culture, and Power in Early Modern China* (Stanford: Stanford University Press, 2004), pp. 19–56. The robustness of traditional Chinese printing methods has now been even more conclusively demonstrated by Joseph P. McDermott, *A Social History of the Chinese Book: Books and Literati Culture in Late Imperial China* (Hong Kong: Hong Kong University Press, 2006), pp. 9–42.

17. The quotation is from p. 243 of Alfred Lister, 'Chinese Almanacs', in *The China Review* 1 (1872–3), pp. 237–44. The word 'cash' here is the English term (originally perhaps from Tamil) for an Asian coin of very low value – here, the round Chinese copper coin with a square hole in the middle.

Etymologically, despite appearances, it has nothing to do with the word 'cash' meaning ready money.

18. Blake Morrison, *The Justification of Johannes Gutenberg* (London: Chatto & Windus, 2000).

19. The outlines of this tale have long been known: cf. Adolf Reichwein, *China and Europe* (London: Routledge & Kegan Paul, 1968, reissue of 1925), pp. 29–31; George Savage, *Porcelain through the Ages* (Harmondsworth: Penguin, 1963), pp. 123–6. For a more up to date summary, see Rose Kerr and Nigel Wood, *Science and Civilization in China*, V.12 (Cambridge: Cambridge University Press, 2004), pp. 749–54.

20. Hobson, *Eastern Origins of Western Civilisation*, p. 185.

21. See the discussion in John Larner, *Marco Polo and the Discovery of the World* (New Haven: Yale University Press, 1999), pp. 118–19.

22. There is a rather fine illustration of this in Andrew Burnett, *Interpreting the Past: Coins* (London: British Museum Press, 1991), pp. 16–17.

23. Note p. 289 of David McKitterick, 'The Beginning of Printing', in Christopher Allmand, ed., *The New Cambridge Medieval History*, Vol. 7: *c.* 1415–1500 (Cambridge: Cambridge University Press, 1998), pp. 287–98.

24. Douglas C. McMurtrie, *The Book: The Story of Printing and Bookmaking* (New York: Oxford University Press, 1943), pp. 108–10; S. A. M. Adshead, *Material Culture in Europe and China, 1400–1800* (London: Macmillan Press, 1997), p. 201, attributes to Christopher de Hamel the assertion that printing came to Europe half a century before Gutenberg, though without specifying just where the assertion is made.

25. T. H. Tsien, *Science and Civilisation in China*, Vol. 5.1 (Cambridge: Cambridge University Press, 1985), p. 313.

26. For more details on the hypothesis that follows concerning the transmission of the idea of movable type printing, see T. H. Barrett, *The Rise and Spread of Printing: A New Account of Religious Factors*, SOAS Working Papers in the Study of Religions (London: SOAS, March 2001), pp. 23–6, and notes, on which my remarks are closely based, except where otherwise indicated. Since this study was not widely distributed, I intend to publish a second edition with addenda and corrigenda in 2008 under the Minnow imprint of London.

27. On this question see Ruth W. Dunnell, *The Great State of White and High* (Honolulu: University of Hawaii Press, 1996), p. 38.

28. It may well be, however, that the fact that wood or woodblock carvers were in short supply was more important. See my comments on Uighur Buddhist printing, below. I have not been able to investigate this problem to my satisfaction, and my interpretations remain entirely tentative.

29. Lynn White, Jr, 'Tibet, India, and Malaya as Sources of Western Medieval Technology', *American Historical Review* 65.3 (1960), pp. 515–26.

30. On printing in the Tangut language in the fourteenth century, see p. 204 of Ruth W. Dunnell, 'The Hsi Hsia', in Herbert Franke and Denis Twitchett,

eds, *The Cambridge History of China*, Vol. 6 (Cambridge: Cambridge University Press, 1994), pp. 154–214.

31. The entire story is now described in Cécile Leung, *Etienne Fourmont (1683–1745): Oriental and Chinese Languages in Eighteenth-century France* (Leuven: Leuven University Press, 2002), pp. 241–6.
32. McMurtrie, *The Book*, p. 136.
33. For a succinct survey, see Man, *Gutenberg*, pp. 154–60.
34. Barbara W. Tuchman, *A Distant Mirror: The Calamitous 14th Century* (London: Macmillan, 1979), p. 335.
35. Morrison, *Justification of Johannes Gutenberg*, p. 52.
36. This aspect of early printing is well treated in Lucien Febvre and Henri-Jean Martin, *The Coming of the Book* (London: Verso Classics, 1997), pp. 248–61.
37. This is from the beginning of Man, *Gutenberg*, pp. 60–5, which outlines the whole episode.
38. Elizabeth L. Eisenstein, *The Printing Press as an Agent of Change* (Cambridge: Cambridge University Press, 1979), p. 53, and n. 38.
39. The criticism may be found in Peter Kornicki, *The Book in Japan* (Leiden: Brill, 1998), pp. 24–5.
40. Many of the scholars who are now publishing work in the field are represented in an important collective volume, Cynthia J. Brokaw and Kai-wing Chow, eds, *Printing and Book Culture in Late Imperial China* (Berkeley: University of California Press, 2005).
41. There is now a succinct non-specialist treatment of this 'Question' in Christopher Cullen, *The Dragon's Ascent* (Hong Kong: PCCW IMS, 2001), pp. 148–51, which may help to explain the very brief account given here.

Chapter Two: A Message from Iraklion

1. Much has been written about the disc, frequently in a highly speculative way. The best presentation of the basic, verifiable information about it that I have found is Louis Godart, *The Phaistos Disc* (n.p.: Editions Itanos, 1995).
2. In considering the early evolution of writing towards printing, the main sources that have been used here for reference are David Diringer, *The Book before Printing: Ancient, Medieval and Oriental* (New York: Dover Publications, 1982 reprint of 1953) and Constance R. Miller, *Technical and Cultural Prerequisites for the Invention of Printing in China and the West* (San Francisco: Chinese Materials Center, 1983).
3. For the book before printing in China, the standard work is Tsuen-hsuin Tsien, *Written on Bamboo and Silk: The Beginnings of Chinese Books and Inscriptions,* 2nd edn (Chicago: Chicago University Press, 2004). For early traces of the brush, see pp. 216–17 of Robert Bagley, 'Anyang Writing and the Origin of the Chinese Writing System', in Stephen D. Houston, ed., *The*

First Writing: Script Invention as History and Process (Cambridge: Cambridge University Press, 2004), pp. 190–249.

4. Robert van Gulik, *The Haunted Monastery and the Chinese Maze Murders: Two Chinese Detective Novels* (New York: Dover Publications, 1977), p. 324, defending the verisimilitude of his novels on the basis of his own experience of Chinese amanuenses.

5. The conclusion on stenography is that of Victor Mair, on p. 91 of his 'Lay Students and the Making of Written Vernacular Narrative: An Inventory of Tun-huang Manuscripts', *Chinoperl Papers* 10 (1981), pp. 5–96, which gives an estimate of the original contents of this archive (first discovered in the late nineteenth century and now scattered across the world's libraries) on pp. 95–6.

6. Bagley, 'Anyang writing', p. 211.

7. *Huainanzi* 8, p. 116, in the edition of the *Zhuzi jicheng* (Beijing: Zhonghua shuja, 1954). The text is from the second century BCE, though the story may be earlier.

8. Mark Edward Lewis, *Writing and Authority in Early China* (Albany: State University of New York Press, 1999), p. 339.

9. A. Warrack, *Chambers's Scots Dialect Dictionary* (London and Edinburgh: W. & R. Chambers, 1911), p. 214.

10. In future any study of early Chinese books will have to take account of the issues raised in Martin Kern, ed., *Text and Ritual in Early China* (Seattle: University of Washington Press, 2005), though to do so here would divert too much attention to what unfortunately can only be treated as 'background', however important it is in its own right.

11. See Imre Galambos, *Orthography of Early Chinese Writing: Evidence from Newly Excavated Manuscripts* (Budapest: Department of East Asian Studies, Eötvös Loránd University, 2006), pp. 35–8, 45, following Wu Hung.

12. The message is shown as an illustration taken from a ceramic vessel in Oliver Moore, *Reading the Past: Chinese* (London: British Museum Press, 2000), p. 58.

13. On this general point, see the perceptive study of Lothar Ledderose, *Ten Thousand Things: Module and Mass Production in Chinese Art* (Princeton: Princeton University Press, 2000), which includes a chapter on the terracotta warriors, and pp. 154–160 on the early background to printing. This feature of the Chinese writing system, initially important for the creation of inscriptions, made the invention of movable type much easier. At a lower level of analysis, of course, Chinese characters themselves may be broken down into 'modules', even when the tendency to make complex characters out of combinations of simpler elements is discounted, since they are formed of a limited repertory of different brush-strokes. This lower level has been of some significance in modern times – for example, as the basis of a form of computer inputting – but seems to have played no discernible part in the early history of Chinese printing. See, however, McDermott, *A*

Social History of the Chinese Book, pp. 25–30, for standardised strokes in later block cutting.

14. Compare H. Gregory Snyder, *Teachers and Text in the Ancient World* (London; Routledge, 2000), pp. 61–3, and Tsien, *Written on Bamboo and Silk*, pp. 78–85.

15. The calculations on Gutenberg's Bible are widely known: see, for example, Man, *Gutenberg*, p. 165.

16. Peter Brown, *The Rise of Western Christendom* (Oxford: Blackwell, 1996), p. 217.

17. The system is described by Ikeda On, 'T'ang Household Registers and Related Documents', in Arthur F. Wright and Denis Twitchett, eds, *Perspectives on the T'ang* (New Haven and London: Yale University Press, 1973), pp. 121–50.

18. For our main source on the events of CE 281, see Deborah Lynn Porter, *From Deluge to Discourse: Myth, History and the Generation of Chinese Fiction* (Albany: State University of New York Press, 1996), pp. 5–7.

19. On Ruan Dan, and reading in general, see Wolfgang Behr and Bernhard Führer, 'Einführende Notizen zum Lesen in China mit besonderer Berücksichtigung der Frühzeit', in Bernhard Führer, ed., *Aspekte des Lesens in China in Vergangheit und Gegenwart* (Bochum: Projekt Verlag, 2005), pp. 1–42, especially pp. 30–1; cf. Alberto Manguel, *A History of Reading* (London: Flamingo, 1997), pp. 41–53 – alas this means no more than 'a history of reading in the West', since China and the rest of the non-Western world scarcely get a mention – who discusses the surprise of St Augustine at meeting the silent reader St Ambrose in 384. Note, too, Arthur Waley, *Ballads and Stories from Tun-huang* (London: George Allen & Unwin, 1960), p. 111, for silent reading as a recognised option mentioned in a popular tale among the Dunhuang manuscripts.

20. Ren Jiyu, ed., *Zhongguo cangshulou* (Shenyang: Liaoning renmin chubanshe, 2001), p. 424.

21. Ibid., p. 429.

22. Ibid., p. 437.

23. Brown, *Rise of Western Christendom*, p. 217.

24. Ouyang Xun, *Yiwen leiju* (Shanghai: Shanghai guji chubanshe, 1982), Foreword, p. 3.

25. Ren, *Zhongguo cangshulou*, p. 501.

26. Richard B. Mather, *The Poet Shen Yüeh (441–513): The Reticent Marquis* (Princeton: Princeton University Press, 1988), p. 170.

27. S. Y. Teng, *Family Instructions for the Yen Clan* (Leiden: E. J. Brill, 1964), p. 54; cf. p. 96, n. 5. The author, Yan Zhitui, lived from 531 to after 591.

28. On this development, see Christopher Leigh Connery, *The Empire of the Text: Writing and Authority in Early Imperial China* (Lanham, MD: Rowman & Littlefield, 1998), which shows the roots of this development under Han autocracy itself.

29. The qualities of this tradition are caught very well in a short work by Stephen Owen, *Remembrances: The Experience of the Past in Classical Chinese Literature* (Cambridge, Mass.: Harvard University Press, 1986).
30. On bookkeeping, see Jack Goody, *The East in the West* (Cambridge: Cambridge University Press, 1996), pp. 49–81.
31. C. R. Bawden, *The Modern History of Mongolia* (London: Kegan Paul International, 1989), pp. 87, 248.

Chapter Three: The Buddha's Word

1. The classic essay on this topic is Richard Gombrich, 'The Significance of the Former Buddhas in the Theravadin Tradition', in Somaratna Balasooriya, André Bareau, Richard Gombrich, Siri Gunasingha, Udaye Mallawarachchi and Edmund Perry, *Buddhist Studies in Honour of Walpola Rahula* (London: Gordon Fraser, 1980), pp. 62–72.
2. This area of study is developing rapidly, but for a particularly lucid survey reflecting the state of knowledge in the 1990s, one may consult K. R. Norman, *A Philological Approach to Buddhism* (London: SOAS, 1997), pp. 41–57.
3. A very useful recent synthesis of scholarship is John S. Strong, *Relics of the Buddha* (Princeton: Princeton University Press, 2004): see the survey of approaches on pp. 4–5.
4. I have argued that this became the case in China in 'The Religious Meaning of Buddhist Sculpture in its Cultural Setting: The Buddha Images of Qingzhou in the Light of Recent Scholarship', *Buddhist Studies Review* 22.1 (2005), pp. 44–69, but cf. Strong, *Relics*, pp. 18–20, for a distinction between image and relic, albeit one that could be readily eliminated by including relics in images.
5. For an examination of this dictum in the context of notions of who the Buddha was, see the remarks of Guang Xing, *The Concept of the Buddha* (London: RoutledgeCurzon, 2005), p. 72; cf. Strong, *Relics*, pp. 8–10.
6. For the problems of writing on palm leaf, see Diringer, *The Book before Printing*, p. 42; cf. p. 361 for birch bark as a possible alternative, but note that this seems to have been a secondary (and regional) development, formatted to imitate either the Greek papyrus scroll or the Indian palm leaf.
7. This is the first Chinese translation from the 'Perfection of Wisdom' literature, the *Daoxing boruo jing*, 2, p. 436b, Taisho Canon, vol. 8, no. 224.
8. There is a rather inexact Italian translation of the passage on the writing down of the canon in Carlo Puini, *Mahaparinirvana-sutra* (Genova: I Dioscuri, 1990; originally Lanciano, 1911), p. 101; cf. the Chinese original, *Fo banniyuan jing*, 2, p. 175c, in Taisho Canon, vol. 1, no. 5. 'Bamboo and

silk' is in the earliest *Lotus Sutra*: Seishi Karashima, *A Glossary of Dharmarakṣa's Translation of the Lotus Sutra* (Tokyo: International Research Institute for Advanced Buddhology, Soka University, 1998), p. 418, identifies the original Sanskrit for the word translated 'copy' or 'write', but not the material specified.

9. For a study of the note on this Buddhist text and the historical circumstances it describes, see Tokiwa Daijō, *Go-Kan yori SōSei ni itaru yakkyō sōroku* (Tokyo: Tōhō gakuin, 1938), pp. 681–2.

10. On the miracle tale literature, see Robert Ford Campany, *Strange Writing: Anomaly Accounts in Early Medieval China* (Albany: State University of New York Press, 1996), especially pp. 324–5 and 334 for sutra-related miracles, for which further information may be found in his earlier work cited there.

11. W. J. F. Jenner, *Memories of Loyang: Yang Hsüan-chih and the Lost Capital (493–534)* (Oxford: Clarendon Press, 1981), p. 232. As Antonello Palumbo has pointed out to me, it is not immediately obvious what was in the containers by this point.

12. For an example of the first sort, see e.g. the illustration of Pelliot ms. no. 2168 in Pauline Yu, Peter Bol, Stephen Owen and Willard Peterson, *Ways with Words: Writing about Reading Texts from Early China* (Berkeley and Los Angeles: University of California Press, 2000), p. 115, and of the second, Bunsaku Kurata and Yoshiro Tamura, eds, *Art of the Lotus Sutra: Japanese Masterpieces* (Tokyo: Kosei, 1987), illustration 68.

13. See the illustration on p. 149 of Paul Groner, 'Icons and Relics in Eison's Religious Activities', in Robert H. Sharf and Elizabeth Horton Sharf, eds, *Living Images: Japanese Buddhist Icons in Context* (Honolulu: University of Hawaii Press, 2001), pp. 114–50, and, for some further discussion, Barrett, 'Religious Meaning of Buddhist Sculpture in its Cultural Setting', pp. 60–2.

14. Monika Drexler, *Daoistische Schriftmagie: Interpretationen zu den Schriftamuletten Fu im Daozang* (Stuttgart: Steiner, 1994).

15. Michel Strickmann, *Chinese Magical Medicine* (Stanford: Stanford University Press, 2002), pp. 123–93.

16. Richard B. Mather, *Shih-shuo hsin-yü: A New Account of Tales of the World*, 2nd edn (Ann Arbor: Center for Chinese Studies, University of Michigan, 2002), p. 388.

17. The latest study known to me is T. Moriyasu, 'Chronologie des sceaux officiels employés par les commissaires impériaux de l'Armée Revenue au Devoir', *Studies on the Inner Asian Languages* 15 (2000), pp. 100–13. This is actually just the summary of a much longer article in Japanese, preceded by fifteen plates of photographs of seals and followed by a definitive catalogue, albeit one that only covers less than a century and a half of documents.

18. Zhisheng, *Kaiyuan shijiao lu* 6, p. 536a, in the edition of the Taisho Canon, vol. 55 – a reference I owe to Antonello Palumbo.

19. Cf. Isabelle Robinet, *Taoist Meditation: The Mao-shan Tradition of Great Purity* (Albany, NY: SUNY, 1993), pp. 21–4.

20. See p. 65 of Yoshiko Kamitsuka, 'Lao-tzu in Six Dynasties Taoist Sculpture', in Livia Kohn and Michael LaFargue, eds, *Lao-tzu and the Tao-te-ching* (Albany, NY: SUNY, 1998), pp. 63–83, though the hostile nature of this source renders it slightly suspect.

21. See Robert Ford Campany, *To Live as Long as Heaven and Earth: A Translation and Study of Ge Hong's Traditions of Divine Transcendents* (Berkeley and Los Angeles: University of California Press, 2002), p. 192.

22. For example in the *Exegesis of the Mahayana*, a text apparently written in eighth-century Korea: See Robert E. Buswell, Jr, *The Formation of Ch'an Ideology in China and Korea* (Princeton: Princeton University Press, 1989), p. 98.

23. Jean-Pierre Drège, *Les Bibliothèques en Chine au temps des manuscripts* (Paris: EFEO, 1991), pp. 197–8.

24. Elizabeth L. Eisenstein, *The Printing Revolution in Early Modern Europe*, 2nd edn (Cambridge: Cambridge University Press, 2005), p. 321, referring to the figures given in Febvre and Martin, *The Coming of the Book*, p. 28.

25. Drège, *Les Bibliothèques en Chine*, p. 199.

26. Fabrizio Pregadio, *Great Clarity: Daoism and Alchemy in Early Medieval China* (Stanford: Stanford University Press, 2006), pp. 91–2.

27. James R. Ware, *Alchemy, Medicine and Religion in the China of AD 320: The Nei P'ien of Ko Hung* (Cambridge, Mass.: MIT Press, 1966), pp. 298, 299, though this translation does not bring out the reference to clay in the original.

Chapter Four: The Ruin of Britain

1. The material for this chapter is drawn unless otherwise noted from my text for the thirty-seventh Evans-Wentz lecture at Stanford University in May 2006, on 'Religion and Climate Change', now published as 'Climate Change and Religious Response: The Case of Early Medieval China' *Journal of the Royal Asiatic Society*, third series, 17.2 (April 2007), pp. 139–56.

2. For my lecture at Stanford I took as my point of departure for discussion of the 536 event a book by archaeological journalist David Keys, *Catastrophe: An Investigation into the Origins of the Modern World* (London: Century, 1999). This, however, overlooks such pioneering work as R. B. Stothers, 'Mystery Cloud of AD 536', *Nature* 307 (January 1984), pp. 344–5. For evidence relating his more recent work to East Asia, see Rosanne D'Arrigo, David Frank, Gordon Jacoby and Neil Pederson, 'Spatial Response to Major Volcanic Events in or about AD 536, 934, and 1258: Frost Rings and other

Dendrochronological Evidence from Mongolia and Northern Siberia: Comment on R. B. Stothers, "Volcanic Dry Fogs, Climate Cooling, and Plague Pandemics in Europe and the Middle East" (Climate Change 42, 1999)', *Climate Change* 49.1–2 (April 2001), pp. 239–48.

3. Fang Xiaoyang, Zhang Binglun and Fan Jialu, '"Yuyin yubanshu" yu diaoban yinshua shu faming de jishu guanlian', *Zhongguoshi yanjiu* (2002.1), p. 174. I am most grateful to John Moffett for bringing this report to my attention.

4. Tsien, *Written on Bamboo and Silk*, pp. 92–5, discusses 'ink squeezes'. For the use of rubbings in parallel with printing, see Wu Hung, 'On Rubbings: Their Materiality and Historicity', in Judith T. Zeitlin and Lydia H. Liu, eds, *Writing and Materiality in China: Essays in Honor of Patrick Hanan* (Cambridge, Mass.: Harvard University Press, 2003), pp. 29–72.

5. The process whereby Gong's activities entered the existing historical record in the biography of the official who eventually stopped them is unknown, and was probably quite complex, but we may presume an initial process of editing in the sixth century before the existing accounts were definitively compiled in the seventh.

6. This site, though mentioned in a number of publications, is currently the object of a major research project being undertaken by Lothar Ledderose.

7. Note James O. Caswell, *Written and Unwritten: A New History of the Buddhist Caves at Yungang* (Vancouver: UBC Press, 1988): pp. 67–8, shows that for the first phase of cave building the author still accepts this interpretation of the iconography, even though he prefers not to apply it to later developments at the site.

8. On this episode, see Andreas Janousch, 'The Emperor as Bodhisattva: The Bodhisattva Ordination and Ritual Assemblies of Emperor Wu of the Liang Dynasty', in Joseph P. McDermott, ed., *State and Court Ritual in China* (Cambridge: Cambridge University Press, 1999), pp. 112–49.

9. For a succinct summary of this conception in general in relation to Buddhism, see Steve Collins, *Nirvana and Other Buddhist Felicities* (Cambridge: Cambridge University Press, 1998), pp. 470–6, and in relation to the Ashoka legend in particular John S. Strong, *The Legend of King Aśoka* (Princeton: Princeton University Press, 1983), pp. 44–56.

10. Debate on the topic has, however, begun in Chinese publications: see the review by Lin Yunrou of Gu Chengmei, *Cong Tianwang chuantong dao Fowang chuantong: Zhongguo zhongshi Fojiao zhiguo yishi xingtai yanjiu* (Taibei: Shangzhou chubanshe, 2003), in *Tang yanjiu* 10 (2004), pp. 589–98. See now, however, Eugene Wang, *Shaping the Lotus Sutra: Buddhist Visual Culture in Medieval China* (Seattle: University of Washington Press, 2005), pp. 125–6

11. Later anti-Buddhist historians tended to decry the Ashokan pretensions of the Emperor Wu of the Liang dynasty and point to his unfortunate end,

but it is quite evident that under the dynasty that supplanted his, rulers continued to use Ashokan symbolism even so.

12. For a full study of the episode, see Chen Jinhua, *Monks and Monarchs, Kinship and Kingship: Tanqian in Sui Buddhism and Politics* (Kyoto: Italian School of East Asian Studies, 2002), pp. 51–107.

13. See Ningxia wenwu kaogu yanjiusuo, ed., *Baisigou Xixia fangta* (Beijing: Wenwu chubanshe, 2005), p. 393, and illustrations, p. 394, for miniature stupas bearing a pattern of 108 even smaller stupas.

14. The extraordinary story of the forfeiture of such a promising dynastic start is now detailed in Victor Cunrui Xiong, *Emperor Yang of the Sui Dynasty: His Life, Times, and Legacy* (Albany: State University of New York Press, 2006).

15. I have explored these ideas elsewhere, primarily in *Taoism under the T'ang: Religion and Empire during the Golden Age of Chinese History* (London: WellSweep, 1996) and in 'Shinto and Taoism in Early Japan', in John Breen and Mark Teeuwen, eds, *Shinto in History: Ways of the Kami* (Richmond: Curzon Press, 2000), pp. 13–31.

16. James Legge, *A Record of Buddhistic Kingdoms* (Oxford: Clarendon Press, 1886), p. 17.

17. There exists a considerable body of scholarship linked to these objects, brought together expertly by Stanley K. Abe, *Ordinary Images* (Chicago: Chicago University Press, 2002), pp. 103–71.

18. Dorothy C. Wong, *Chinese Steles: Pre-Buddhist and Buddhist Use of a Symbolic Form* (Honolulu: University of Hawaii Press, 2004), pp. 106, 140.

19. Ibid., pp. 73–5.

20. Abe, *Ordinary Images*, p. 100; T. H. Barrett, 'Images of Printing in Seventh Century Chinese Religious Literature', *Chinese Science* 15 (1998), pp. 81–93.

21. Sarah E. Fraser, *Performing the Visual: The Practice of Buddhist Wall Painting in China and Central Asia, 618–960* (Stanford: Stanford University Press, 2004), pp. 98, 102–8.

22. Shi Yunli, 'Xin gongkaide Dunhuang Nan Qi xieben shang de nayin Foxiang', *Zhongguo yinshua niankan* (Beijing: Zhonguo yinshua niankan she, 2001), p. 407.

23. For a brief summary drawing on the work of Daniel Boucher and others, see Abe, *Ordinary Images*, pp. 160–2, and note on the last page Abe's suggestion that the formula functioned as what I term a 'spell'. For the suggested dating in the light of Japanese Indological scholarship, see Barrett, *The Rise and Spread of Printing*, p. 9 and n. 44, and also p. 13, n. 27 of T. H. Barrett, 'Stūpa, Sūtra and Śarīra in China, c. 656–706 CE', *Buddhist Studies Review* 18.1 (2001), pp. 1–64.

24. See Gregory Schopen, *Figments and Fragments of Mahayana Buddhism in India: More Collected Papers* (Honolulu: University of Hawaii Press, 2005), pp. 203–4 (cf. the translations into Chinese listed on p. 207) and

the study reprinted on pp. 314–44: note again the references to China on p. 337.

25. Schopen, ibid., pp. 350–69, reports Indian and Tibetan practice in this regard, but only Niu Dasheng seems to have commented on Chinese material (see n. 27 below), and he in his turn is unaware of Schopen's work.

26. We have not discussed change in Europe, but Gildas, to take just one example, is truly remarkable not for his rambling jeremiads but for having spurred a great movement towards monasticism in Celtic Christianity.

27. See the very useful survey by Niu Dasheng in Ningxia wenwu kaogu yanjiusuo, ed., *Baisigou Xixia fangta* (Beijing: Wenwu chubanshe, 2005), pp. 391–415, with copious illustration. On p. 399 the author lists Tang examples of moulded funerary miniature Buddha images with added inscriptions, and cf. p. 396 and the illustrations on p. 398.

28. On this list, see T. H. Barrett, 'The *Feng-tao k'o* and Printing on Paper in Seventh-century China', *Bulletin of the School of Oriental and African Studies* 60.3 (1997), pp. 538–40: this study shows that it cannot be later than the middle of the seventh century, but I am now disposed to think that it cannot be much earlier either.

Chapter Five: The Lives and Loves of the Li Family

1. See p. 90 of Denis Twitchett, '*How to Be an Emperor:* T'ang T'ai-tsung's Vision of his Role', *Asia Major*, third series, 9.1–2 (1996), pp. 1–102. The dynastic events described in the following pages are drawn mainly from Denis Twitchett, ed., *The Cambridge History of China, Vol. 3: Sui and T'ang China, 581–907 AD* (Cambridge: Cambridge University Press, 1979), Chapters 3–6.

2. For one recent tribute to the monk and his travels, see Sun Shuyun, *Ten Thousand Miles without a Cloud* (London: Harper Perennial, 2004).

3. See p. 262 of Arthur F. Wright, 'T'ang T'ai-tsung and Buddhism', in Arthur F. Wright and Denis Twitchett, eds, *Perspectives on the T'ang* (New Haven and London: Yale University Press, 1973), pp. 239–63.

4. For the original source and translations on this matter, see pp. 10–12 of T. H. Barrett, 'Stūpa', pp. 1–64, and pp. 35–6 of Jinhua Chen, Śarīra and Scepter: Empress Wu's Political Use of Buddhist Relics', *Journal of the International Association of Buddhist Studies* 25.1–2 (2002), pp. 33–150, from which two studies much of what follows is drawn.

5. Cf. Barrett, 'Stūpa', pp. 13–14; Chen, 'Śarīra', p. 45.

6. Note, however, that S. P. Chatterjee, *The Mission of Wang Hiuen Ts'e in India* (Delhi: Sri Satguru Publications, 1987), pp. 21–2, which is based on a translation of the early French research of Sylvain Levi, renders this as 'impressions of the Buddha', which would suggest that he took the phrase to indicate the products of stamping rather than the stamps.

7. Niu, in *Baishigou Xi Xia fangta*, p. 399.

8. For the images, see Barrett, 'Stūpa', pp. 11–12, n. 25.

9. The narrative that follows is largely based on the revisionist approach found in R. W. L. Guisso, *Wu Tse-t'ien and the Politics of Legitimation in T'ang China* (Bellingham, Wash.: Western Washington University, 1978).

10. Barrett, *Taoism under the T'ang*, pp. 44–5.

11. See the arguments of Han Sheng on p. 51 of his study 'Wu Zetian de jiashi yu shengnian', in Wang Wenchao and Zhao Wenrun, eds, *Wu Zetian yu Songshan* (Beijing: Zhonghua shuju, 2003), pp. 45–54.

12. See the materials collected in Zhang Zexian, ed., *Tang Wudai nongmin zhanzheng shiliao huibian* (Beijing: Zhonghua shuju, 1979), pp. 21–5.

13. Barrett, *Taoism under the T'ang*, pp. 29–30.

14. Besides the two articles already cited by myself, 'Stūpa' and (in more detail) Jinhua Chen, *Śarīra*, on the political use of relics by the empress, there is also a useful account of this cult centre and its background in Tansen Sen, *Buddhism, Diplomacy, and Trade: The Realignment of Sino-Indian Relations, 600–1400* (Honolulu: University of Hawaii Press, 2003), pp. 55–68.

15. Again, Sen, *Buddhism, Diplomacy, and Trade*, pp. 76–86, provides a useful general view.

16. In my earlier work on Tang Taoist ideology I overlooked this fact: see, however, p. 66 and p. 74, n. 51 of Stephen R. Bokenkamp, 'The Peach Flower Font and the Grotto Passage', *Journal of the American Oriental Society* 106 (1986), pp. 65–79, which mentions her title in an earlier Taoist scripture under the translations 'Empress of Heaven' and 'Consort of Heaven'.

17. On this point Jinhua Chen's article adduces evidence that corrects my earlier work, which relied only on sources discovered by Antonino Forte: these, however, do indicate a more than merely internal distribution of relics, following the pattern we have noted under the preceding dynasty.

18. Compare Zhiyi, *Miaofa lianhua jing wenju* 8, p. 111a1, in the edition of the Taisho Canon, no. 1718 in vol. 34, and Fabrizio Pregadio, *Great Clarity: Daoism and Alchemy in Early Medieval China* (Stanford: Stanford University Press, 2006), p. 87.

19. Barrett, *Taoism under the T'ang*, pp. 44–5; Han Sheng, in Wang and Zhao, *Wu Zetian yu Songshan*, p. 51.

20. The reader of Chinese will actually find a good number of explanations of her conduct put forward in the various contributions to Wang and Zhao, *Wu Zetian yu Songshan*.

21. For a recent summary of the problems surrounding what we know of this episode, see Imre Galambos, 'Dunhuang Characters and the Dating of Manuscripts', in Susan Whitfield, ed., *The Silk Road: Trade, Travel, War and Faith* (London: The British Library, 2004), pp. 72–80.

22. See p. 97 of Rob Linrothe, 'Xia Renzong and the Patronage of Tangut Buddhist Art', *Journal of Sung-Yuan Studies* 28 (1998), pp. 91–121.

23. The text in question is touched on in the articles on ruling and relics by myself and Jinhua Chen, and apparently in unpublished work by the late Antonino Forte as well, to judge from his remarks in the posthumously published revised edition of his *Political Propaganda and Ideology in China at the End of the Seventh Century* (Kyoto: ISEAS, 2005), pp. 25–8 and p. 142, n. 240. For now much can already be gleaned concerning this work from the elegant and erudite study by Paul Kroll, *Dharma Bell and Dharani Pillar* (Kyoto: ISEAS, 2001), pp. 39–75, which translates a piece by Li Bai relating to the text. The reference to rubbings (first noticed by Zhou Yiliang) is in Wang Chang, *Jinhua cuibian* (Shanghai: Saoye shanfang, 1921), p. 66.9a. Text P.4501 among the Dunhuang manuscripts of Paris shows that one version of the work was printed by the late tenth century.

24. Statistics quoted on p. 19 of Qiao Fengqi, 'Wu Zetian yu Dengfeng', in Wang and Zhao, *Wu Zetian yu Songshan*, pp. 17–20.

Chapter Six: A Woman Alone

1. Cf. Cao Zhi, *Zhongguo yinshuashu de qiyuan* (Wuhan: Wuhan daxue chubanshe, 1994), p. 515; Pan Jixing, *Zhongguo, Hanguo yu Ouzhou zaoqi yinshuashu de bijiao* (Beijing: Kexue chubanshe, 1997), pp. 45–6.

2. Li Su, *Da Tang xinyu* 9 (Beijing: Zhonghua shuju, 1984), p. 142; Sima Guang , *Zizhi tongjian* 204 (Beijing: Zhonghua shuju, 1957), p. 6475 – note the discussion of sources in the commentary. For a manuscript authorisation with a seal stamped on it another term, *yinxin* ('seal-letter') was used – this term is frequently found in connection with the catalogues of Buddhist texts brought back by Japanese monks from China in the early ninth century, for reasons we shall discuss in Chapter Eight.

3. Strickmann, *Chinese Magical Medicine*, pp. 170–8. Of course, if 'seal-paper' was already being used as a form of security pass at the time of the writing of this text (and of the other similar but later materials where the term occurs), then this would enhance our understanding of the religious rituals described, especially in view of the traditional Chinese tendency to see the afterlife as dominated by a vast and hellish bureaucracy.

4. I have noted this passage in T. H. Barrett, 'Woodblock Dyeing and Printing Technology in China, *c.* 700 AD: The Innovations of Ms. Liu, and Other Evidence', *Bulletin of the School of Oriental and African Studies* 64.2 (2001), pp. 240–7. The fullest discussion of the sources (including many later sources) on *yinzhi* outside religious contexts is in Cao, *Zhongguo yinshuashu de qiyuan*, pp. 276–81.

5. This matter is discussed in T. H. Barrett, 'Evidence for 7th Century Taoist Printing', *Needham Research Institute Newsletter* 17 (December 1998),

p.[5]; I intend to return to it in a more extended study of Taoism and printing in future.

6. The following account is based on T. H. Barrett, 'Did I-Ching Go to India? Problems in Using I-Ching as a Source on South Asian Buddhism', *Buddhist Studies Review* 15.2 (1998), pp. 142–56; reprinted in Paul Williams, ed., *Buddhism: Critical Concepts in Religious Studies* 7 (London: Routledge, 2006), pp. 1–12. For the chronology of Yijing's life this study relied on the research of Wang Bangwei. Yijing does elsewhere offer third-hand testimony suggesting that the cult of the miniature stupa was seeing a considerable vogue in India: one king is alleged to have been responsible for 100,000 items daily. Cf. Latika Lahiri, *Chinese Monks in India* (Delhi: Motilal Banarsidass, 1986), p. 85, translating from Taisho Canon vol. 51, text no. 2066, 2, p. 8c3.

7. See the discussion in Wang Bangwei, *Tang Gaoseng Yijing shengping ji qi zhuzuo lunkao* (Chongqing: Chongqing chubanshe, 1996), p. 16.

8. These indications were expertly reviewed on pp. 278–81 of Antonino Forte, 'The Five Kings of India and the King of Kucha who according to Chinese Sources went to Luoyang in 692', in Raffaele Torella, ed., *Le Paroli e I Marmi: Studi in onore di Raniero Gnoli nel suo 70° compleanno* (Rome: Istituto Italiano per l'Africa e l'Oriente, 2001), pp. 261–83.

9. Eugene Wang, *Shaping the Lotus Sutra*, p. 124.

10. The Chinese scholar Tang Yongtong believed that she had thirty-six sets copied, while admitting that the number 'thirty-six' could refer to the subsections of one canon: *Tang Yongtong xuanji* (Changchun: Jilin renmin chubanshe, 2005), pp. 516–19, reprinting an article 'Cong *Yiqie daojing* shuodao Wu Zetian' from *Guangming ribao,* 21 November 1962. Cf. however Liu Yi, 'Research into the Catalogue of the *Daozang* of the Early Tang Dynasty based on *Nanzhu guan ji* and the Daoist Scriptures of Dunhuang', in Poul Andersen and Florian C. Reiter, eds, *Scriptures, Schools, and Forms of Practice in Daoism: A Berlin Symposium* (Wiesbaden: Harrasowitz, 2005), pp. 185–214.

11. See Zanning, *Song Gaoseng zhuan* 25, p. 869c in the edition of the Taisho Canon, vol. 50, text no. 2061.

12. Reference to this vow appears in the commentary on the Buddhist prophecy of female rule produced by her monks to legitimise her change of dynasty. The passage is now translated in Antonino Forte, *Political Propaganda and Ideology,* p. 279, giving the figure as read by Jinhua Chen, '*Śarīra* and Scepter', p. 62, as a vow to create 8,040,000 stupas. I do not see myself that the text states that she had actually fulfilled her vow, though Jinhua Chen reads this to mean that this event had occurred in a previous incarnation. Even in this case, the prophecy implies that she is capable of extraordinary productivity, and there must have been some pressure on her to live up to this image.

13. Su Bai, *Tang-Song shiqi de diaoban yinshua* (Beijing: Wenwu chubanshe, 1999), pp. 6–8, provides a survey of these materials, but does not endorse any specific date, beyond suggesting a sequence of development.
14. The full story of the discovery of the message is given in Li Zhenzhong and Wang Xuebao, 'Wu Zetian jinjian faxian shimo', in Wang and Zhao, *Wu Zetian yu Songshan*, pp. 162–5.
15. For a preliminary translation of an official document to this effect, see pp. 322–3 of T. H. Barrett, 'Inner and Outer Ritual: Some Remarks on a Directive concerning Daoist Dragon-casting Ritual from Dunhuang', in Lee Cheuk Yin and Chan Man Sing, eds, *A Daoist Florilegium: A Festschrift Dedicated to Professor Liu Ts'un-yan on his Eighty-fifth Birthday* (Xianggang: Shangwu yinshuguan, 2002), pp. 315–34. A considerable body of scholarship on the practice has now appeared: for one recent and particularly helpful contribution, see Wang Yucheng, 'Tang Xuanzong toulong tongjian kaoshu', *Hongdao* 10 (2001), pp. 86–91. My thanks to Guo Wu for sending me a copy of this journal.
16. On these elements, see pp. 168–71 of Dong Li, 'Wu Zetian chuzui jinjian kaoshi', in Wang and Zhao, *Wu Zetian yu Songshan*, pp. 166–74.
17. U.-A. Cedzich, 'Corpse Deliverance, Substitute Bodies, Name Change, and Feigned Death: Aspects of Metamorphosis and Immortality in Early Medieval China', *Journal of Chinese Religions* 29 (2001), pp. 1–68.
18. Michael E. Welch, 'Fa-tsang, Pure Light, and Printing: An Inquiry into the Origins of Textual Xylography' (MA Dissertation in Library Science, University of Minnesota, 1981), pp. 101–2. I am extremely grateful to Michael Welch for making a copy of his extraordinary pioneering work available to me, and to Jinhua Chen both for bringing it to my attention and for contacting the author on my behalf. Note also the endorsement of Welch's study in Forte, *Political Propaganda and Ideology*, p. 142, where the contemporary Chinese interest in the theme of women miraculously achieving Buddhist masculinity is now given additional documentation
19. Schopen, *Figments and Fragments*, pp. 204; 219–20, notes 47–8; 259; 337–8.
20. Besides my own work and that of Michael Welch, Peter F. Kornicki, working from the Japanese and Korean materials, concurs in pointing to the ruler of the Great Zhou as having in all likelihood provided a model for the rest of East Asia: cf. his monograph *The Book in Japan: A Cultural History from the Beginnings to the Nineteenth Century* (Leiden: Brill, 1998), pp. 114–17. Note also, in China, Yang Junkai, 'Diaoban yinshua qi yu Zhongguo', *Wenbo* 3 (2000), pp. 31–8, a reference reviewing the circumstantial evidence for printing at this time kindly retrieved for me by Glen Dudbridge from the files of the late Piet van der Loon.
21. E. g. a copy of the *Lotus Sutra* now in Japan, though Denis Twitchett, *Printing and Publishing in Medieval China* (London: Wynkyn de Worde

Society, 1983), p. 89, hesitates to endorse any exact date, given that the usage of the special characters cannot in the current state of our research be narrowly confined to the period from their introduction to the restoration of the Tang dynasty, especially if the wood-carvers were following an old manuscript exemplar. Cf. Wang Qinruo, ed., *[Songben] Cefu yuangui* (Beijing: Zhonghua shuju, 1989), p. 160.6a, which apparently shows that the special characters were still being used in 837.

22. See her preface to the *Ru ding buding yin jing*, p. 706a, lines 7–8, in Taisho Canon, Vol. 15, text no. 646.

23. See p. 36 of Edmund H. Worthy, Jr, 'Diplomacy for Survival: Domestic and Foreign Relations of Wu Yüeh, 907–78', in Morris Rossabi, ed., *China among Equals* (Berkeley and Los Angeles: University of California Press, 1983), pp.17–44, which refers to more detailed Japanese research. Relic distribution (though not printed relics) remained for a while part of the accession ceremonies of the Japanese imperial tradition: cf. Ryuichi Abe, *The Weaving of Mantra* (New York: Columbia University Press, 1999), p. 367.

24. T. H. Barrett, 'Was There an Imperial Distribution of Relics in Ninth-century China?', *Bulletin of the School of Oriental and African Studies* 68.3 (2005), pp. 451–4.

25. See Linrothe, 'Xia Renzong', and also Ruth W. Dunnell, *The Great State of White and High* (Honolulu: Hawaii University Press, 1996), pp. 92–4, 121. At the time that the king in the lower Yangzi region was distributing his relics, the Tanguts were a disunited people who had yet to form a state of their own, so they would not have been recipients.

26. Ningxia wenwu kaogu yanjiusuo, *Baisigou Xi Xia fangta*, pp. 401–8.

Chapter Seven: Of Monks and Mysteries

1. The following account of Fazang draws very largely on Jinhua Chen's monograph from E. J. Brill on his life and political career, *Philosopher, Practitioner, Politician: The Many Lives of Fazang (643–712)*, (Leiden, Boston: Brill, 2007). I am most grateful to Professor Chen for taking up this tricky topic in his own research, since this has made my task much easier.

2. In his *Huayan jing zhuanji* 5, p. 171a, b in the edition of the Taisho Canon, vol. 51, text no. 2073. These references I owe to Jinhua Chen's forthcoming study.

3. For a demonstration of this, see Eugene Wang, 'Oneiric Horizon and Dissolving Bodies: Buddhist Cave Shrine as Mirror Hall', *Art History* 24.4 (2004), pp. 494–521.

4. Jiro Sugiyama, 'The Stone Sculptures of Pao-ch'ing Temple Revisited', *Journal of the International College for Advanced Buddhist Studies* 5 (March 2002),

pp.1–54 (in Japanese; English summary). For this chronology, as in the preceding chapter, I follow Jinhua Chen's article on the political use of relics.

5. Sugiyama, 'Stone Sculptures', pp. 6–7. Chen Zhi, 'Tangdai san ni foxiang', *Wenwu* 8 (1959), pp. 49–51, interprets the phrase as indicating the use of relic ash, though he notes that stroke variations in the inscriptions suggest they were inscribed manually. Schopen, *Figments and Fragments,* Chapter 14, pp. 350–69, is a pioneering study of the Indo-Tibetan background to the practice.

6. Though his most detailed arguments to this end are in his 2007 work, some of the research supporting the foregoing account of Fazang's role may be found in Jinhua Chen, 'More than a Philosopher: Fazang (643–712) as Politician and Miracle-worker', *History of Religion* 42.4 (May 2003), pp. 320–58.

7. In medieval China, the spirits of particularly violent persons were accorded especially wary respect that tended to raise them from the category of mere ancestral spirit to that of god. Cf. Alvin Cohen, 'Coercing the Rain Deities in Ancient China', *History of Religions* 17.3–4 (1979), pp. 244–65, for a fine example of this type.

8. For one explanation of this omission, see Shi Quanrong, Song Jichao, Xi Jiantao and Song Shaoyu, 'Qianling wuzibei xinkao', in Wang and Zhao, *Wu Zetian yu Songshan,* pp. 388–94. From Song times onwards, the pristine condition of the stone has unfortunately been obscured by inscriptions by later hands. My colleague Antonello Palumbo points out that there are Central Asian precedents for the use of a plain memorial monolith, and that the stone came from Khotan: cf. Song Minqiu, *Chang'an zhi* 19.3a, in the *Song-Yuan difangzhi congshu* reprint of the 1787 edition.

9. See p. 182 of David L. McMullen, 'The Death Rites of Tang Daizong', in McDermott, *State and Court Ritual,* pp. 150–96.

10. For her tomb and its environs, see Tonia Eckfield, *Imperial Tombs in Tang China, 618–907: The Politics of Paradise* (London: RoutledgeCurzon, 2005), pp. 19–28, and cf. p. 61 for the scale of building at this time.

11. In all probability, Fazang would have considered forty-nine days the time during which he needed to act to secure a good reincarnation for his patron: cf. Stephen S. Teiser, *The Scripture on the Ten Kings and the Making of Purgatory in Medieval Buddhism* (Honolulu: University of Hawaii Press, 1994), pp. 23–5.

12. The date given in my earlier work on this inscription is a month too late, due to my slipping a line in reading a conversion table.

13. See Antonino Forte, *A Jewel in Indra's Net* (Kyoto: Italian School of East Asian Studies, 2000), p. 68, for his conclusion on the dating of this source.

14. The example of Yijing's translation is noticed by Welch, 'Fa-tsang, Pure Light, and Printing', p. 64. The embassy of May–June might not have had time to send texts back by mid-July, but there had been two embassies in the preceding years also.

15. The following account is based on Barrett, 'Images of Printing in Seventh Century Chinese Religious Literature', pp. 81–93, and T. H. Barrett with Antonello Palumbo, 'The Mystery of the Precious Seal of the Ruler and the Origins of Printing', *Sungkyun Journal of East Asian Studies* 7.1 (April 2007), pp. 115–29.

16. See, for a non-Mahayana reference, Bhikku Nanamoli, trans., *The Path of Purification* (Berkeley, Calif.: Shambhala, 1976, reprint), p. 639. I am indebted to Rupert Gethin of Bristol University for supplying me with this passage.

Chapter Eight: From Concubines to Criminals

1. For Europe, see McMurtrie, *The Book*, p. 131.
2. The opening of this chapter draws on Barrett, 'Woodblock Dyeing'.
3. The priority of India is asserted but not documented in A. Rahman, ed., *India's Interaction with China, Central and West Asia*, History of Science, Philosophy and Culture in Indian Civilisation Vol. 3.2 (New Delhi: Oxford University Press, 2002), p. 365.
4. For example, Noritake Tsuda, *Handbook of Japanese Art* (Rutland, Vermont and Tokyo: Tuttle, 1976; reprint of Tokyo: Sanseido, 1941), p. 58.
5. The edict is noted in Barrett, *Taoism under the T'ang*, p. 56; for the number of households, see Twitchett, *Cambridge History of China*, Vol. 3, p. 419.
6. See Chen Zhichao, 'Tang Xuanzong *Daode jing zhu* zhu wenti', *Shijie zongjiao yanjiu* (1988.3), pp. 146–50: note especially p. 148 on the failure to use printing and p. 150 on the link between one 'standard' manuscript and the civil service examination system.
7. In giving more weight to these larger questions than my narrow focus on religion and printing initially allowed, I am following the advice of Antonello Palumbo, whose late teacher, Antonino Forte, did much throughout a career of brilliant research to establish the uniqueness of the cultural environment of the late seventh century. Future research into the history of printing may well show that this cosmopolitan phase with its rapid pace of technological advance was a more important background to innovation than my own emphasis on specifically religious factors has been able to demonstrate.
8. Eckfield, *Imperial Tombs*, pp. 23–4.
9. See p. 32 of Tonami Mamoru, 'Policy towards the Buddhist Church in the Reign of T'ang Hsüan-tsung', *Acta Asiatica* 55 (1988), pp. 27–47.
10. See Teiser, *Scripture on the Ten Kings*, p. 98, for a discussion of manuscripts taken from this commercial product. Seo Tatsuhiko, at the end of his very useful catalogue of examples of Tang printing, table 3 on pp. 30–2 of his article 'The Printing Industry in Chang'an's Eastern Market in the Tang

Dynasty', *Memoirs of the Research Department of the Toyo Bunko* 61 (2003), pp. 1–42, follows earlier bibliographers in giving the date of S. 5965, one of the manuscripts concerned, as 902. Teiser gives a slightly later date.

11. Jinhua Chen, 'A Daoist Princess and a Buddhist Temple: A New Theory on the Causes of the Canon-delivering Mission Originally Proposed by Princess Jinxian (689–732) in 730', *Bulletin of the School of Oriental and African Studies* 69.2 (2006), pp. 267–92.

12. See p. 52 of Erik Zürcher, 'Buddhism and Education in T'ang Times', in Wm Theodore de Bary and John W. Chaffee, eds, *Neo-Confucian Education: The Formative Stage* (Berkeley and Los Angeles: University of California Press, 1989), pp. 19–56.

13. For a full list of nearly two hundred monasteries in the imperial capital – not all of which were active at the same time – see Victor Cunrui Xiong, *Sui-Tang Chang'an: A Study in the Urban History of Medieval China* (Ann Arbor: Center for Chinese Studies, University of Michigan, 2000), pp. 303–20.

14. Wang Pu, *Tang huiyao* 41 (Shanghai: Shanghai guji, 1991), p. 873.

15. Cf. Dou Meng's notes to the 'Shu shu fu', in Zhang Yanyuan, ed., *Fashu yaolu* 5 (Shanghai: Shanghai shuhua chubanshe, 1986), p. 142; Zhao Zhenxin, ed., *Fengshi wenjianji jiaozheng* 8 (Peiping: Harvard-Yenching Institute, 1933), p. 5. Though this inscription has been discussed by a number of scholars, perhaps their studies should be reviewed in the light of what follows below.

16. The entire story is provided with full documentation in David McMullen, *State and Scholars in T'ang China* (Cambridge: Cambridge University Press, 1988), pp. 97–100.

17. In July 2004 I presented a paper on 'Tang Monasteries and the Dissemination of Printed Text' at a conference on Buddhist monasticism in East Asia at St John's College, Cambridge covering the details of the episode treated below, but this will require substantial revision before publication.

18. For this general background, see Wang Zhenping, *Ambassadors from the Islands of Immortals* (Honolulu: University of Hawaii Press, 2005), pp. 192–201.

19. Note Kornicki, *The Book in Japan*, p. 285, and p. 81 for the production of manuscripts in Japan, and see R. McKitterick, ed., *Carolingian Culture: Emulation and Innovation* (Cambridge: Cambridge University Press, 1994), pp. 237 and 35, respectively.

20. On this nervousness, see Wang, *Ambassadors*, pp. 197–8.

21. E. O. Reischauer, *Ennin's Diary: The Record of a Pilgrimage to China* (New York: Ronald Press, 1955), pp. 229–30, 236–7. Elsewhere in this source, the purchase or transcription of Buddhist texts does not obviously appear to have taken place on the 'open market', but within Buddhist institutions: cf. pp. 48, 83.

22. I am grateful to Professor Jo-shui Chen for calling my attention to the great disparity in rank between this man and the persons whose correspondence the Great Master chose to preserve with his lists of book titles.
23. The date of the document is preserved in Wang Qinruo, ed., *[Songben] Cefu yuangui*, p. 160.5b.
24. This fragment, and other surviving early printed calendars, are treated on pp. 86 and 94–5 of Alain Arrault and Jean-Claude Martzloff, 'Calendriers', in Marc Kalinowski, ed., *Divination et société dans la Chine médiévale* (Paris: Bibliothèque nationale de France, 2003), pp. 85–211. My thanks to the editor for the gift of this extremely useful reference work.
25. The loyalist's report is summarised in Stanley Weinstein, *Buddhism under the T'ang* (Cambridge: Cambridge University Press, 1987), pp. 60–1.
26. Cao, *Zhongguo yinshuashu de qiyuan*, p. 273 (though the date of 1068 in the source cited is not unambiguously the date when the printing of ordination certificates started); Jacques Gernet, trans. Franciscus Verellen, *Buddhism in Chinese Society: An Economic History from the Fifth to the Tenth Centuries* (New York: Columbia University Press, 1995), pp. 55–6.
27. Cf. T. H. Barrett, 'Buddhist Precepts in a Lawless World', in William M. Bodiford, ed., *Going Forth: Visions of Buddhist Vinaya* (Honolulu: University of Hawaii Press, 2005), pp. 101–23.
28. T. H. Barrett, 'Religion and the First Recorded Print Run: Luoyang, July, 855', *Bulletin of the School of Oriental and African Studies* 68.3 (2005), pp. 455–61.
29. The following remarks are based primarily on Tsien, *Science and Civilisation in China* 5.1, pp. 151–4, plus Seo, 'The Printing Industry'.
30. E.g. one medical text transcribed from a block print is described as part of Vivienne Lo, 'Quick and Easy Chinese Medicine: The Dunhuang Moxibustion Charts', in Vivienne Lo and Christopher Cullen, eds, *Medieval Chinese Medicine: The Dunhuang Medical Manuscripts* (Abingdon: RoutledgeCurzon, 2005), pp. 227–51.
31. See Richard L. Davis, trans., *Historical Records of the Five Dynasties* (New York: Columbia University Press, 2004), p. 454.

Chapter Nine: Filling in the Blanks

1. One good example would be Cao, *Zhongguo yinshuashi de qiyuan*, which is particularly thorough.
2. For a story to this effect, see T. H. Barrett, *Li Ao: Buddhist, Taoist or Neo-Confucian?* (Oxford: Oxford University Press, 1992), p. 42.
3. There is an example of this in Valentina Georgieva, 'Representation of Buddhist Nuns in Chinese Edifying Miracle Tales during the Six Dynasties and the Tang', *Journal of Chinese Religions* 24 (1996), pp. 47–76.

4. See Etienne Balazs, 'History as a Guide to Bureaucratic Practice', in his *Chinese Civilization and Bureaucracy* (New Haven and London: Yale University Press, 1964), pp. 129–49.

5. This has been shown by Rong Xinjiang, 'The Nature of the Dunhuang Library Cave and the Reason for its Sealing', *Cahiers d'Extrême-Asie* 11 (1999–2000), pp. 247–75, though the consequences of his research for the assessment of early printing have yet to be explored. Rong does comment, however, that unfortunately there is no evidence for an intriguing possibility put forward by Fujieda Akira – that the manuscripts were abandoned precisely because they had been supplanted by a complete printed canon dispatched from the capital.

6. The observation is that of Zürcher, 'Buddhism and Education', p. 55.

7. The quotation is from Colin A. Ronan, *The Shorter Science and Civilisation in China*, Vol. 1 (Cambridge: Cambridge University Press, 1978), p. 265.

8. Needham's interpretation of Taoism is questioned by Nathan Sivin's study 'Taoism and Science', in his *Medicine, Philosophy and Religion in Ancient China* (Aldershot: Variorum, 1995), essay VII.

9. Ronan, *Shorter Science and Civilisation in China*, Vol. 1, p. 84.

10. See Barrett, *Li Ao*, pp. 149–50.

11. This engaging custom persisted even after the spread of printing: see Judith T. Zeitlin, 'Disappearing Verses: Writing on Walls and Anxieties of Loss', in Zeitlin and Liu, *Writing and Materiality in China*, pp. 73–132.

12. The classic reconstruction from literature of the ideal high-flying career, by Sun Guodong, is reprinted in his *Tang-Song shi lunji* (Xianggang: Shangwu yinshuguan, 2000), pp. 17–36.

13. The function of this printed slip is explained in Dennis Hirota, *No Abode: The Record of Ippen* (Honolulu: University of Hawaii Press, 1997), pp. xxix–xxxv; the figure is given on p. xxxii, and the slip is reproduced on p. 1.

14. Since Peter Kornicki is primarily concerned with the history of the book, Ippen's printing activities are not discussed in his study.

15. Lin Lu-tche, trans. Robert des Rotours, *Le Règne de l'Empereur Hiuan-tsong (713–756)* (Paris: Collège de France, IHEC, 1981), especially Chapters 2 and 7.

16. Though for the motivation of the earliest historians I rely simply on my own speculation, the summary here draws both on Denis Twitchett, *The Writing of Official History under the T'ang* (Cambridge: Cambridge University Press, 1992), pp. 198, 200 (and cf. p. 143), and on unpublished work by Valentina Boretti, to whom I am most grateful for her help.

17. On this, see T. H. Barrett, 'The Date of the *Leng-chia shih-tzu chi*', *Journal of the Royal Asiatic Society*, third series 1.2 (July 1991), pp. 255–9.

18. Eisenstein, *The Printing Press as an Agent of Change*, p. 54.

19. Certainly not in Great Britain, where the number of trained British researchers under forty capable of reading the sources is probably in single figures, as almost everyone prefers the far quicker returns on learning Mandarin for business purposes.

INDEX